The
Advertising
Agency
Business

The
Advertising
Agency
Business

The Complete Manual for Management & Operation

Herbert S. Gardner, Jr.

NTC Business Books
a division of *NTC Publishing Group* • Lincolnwood, Illinois USA

1989 Printing

Published by NTC Business Books,
a division of NTC Publishing Group,
4255 West Touhy Avenue,
Lincolnwood (Chicago), Illinois 60646-1975 U.S.A.
Manufactured in the United States of America.
Library of Congress Catalog Card Number: 87-82614

9 0 BC 9 8 7 6 5 4 3 2

Dedication

This book is dedicated to the members of the two agency networks which the author managed for some eight years. The opportunity to work with them in solving problems common to most agencies provided the background material for many of the points made in this book. Though they are not identified by name, almost every one of them is included in one connection or another. Without their wholehearted cooperation, this book would not have been possible.

About the Author

Herbert S. Gardner, Jr., one of the sons of Herbert S. Gardner who founded Gardner Advertising Company in St. Louis in 1901, has been involved with the advertising agency business his entire life.

After graduating from Princeton University and doing graduate work in business administration at Massachusetts Institute of Technology, Mr. Gardner joined the Gardner agency first in New York and then in St. Louis.

Concentrating on financial and administrative aspects, he helped develop and modernize a complete package of employee benefits which included a pension plan, a profit-sharing plan, an employee stock-ownership plan, and a diversified insurance program.

After 28 years at Gardner, he joined the management consulting firm of Rubel, Rich & Humphrey in Chicago, where he was involved in management studies for a large number of agencies whose billings ranged from less than $1 million to more than $200 million.

From the Rubel organization Mr. Gardner moved to one of their clients (Basford, Inc.) as chief financial officer.

He then turned to the management of agency networks, serving first as Managing Director of Affiliated Advertising Agencies International, and later assuming the position of Executive Vice-President of First Advertising Agency Network, from which he retired in 1980.

Contents

Introduction and Commercial

The word "commercial" is deliberately included in this preface because the purpose of this book is to sell a concept—that an advertising agency is truly a business, not just a group of hucksters or showmen, as many people believe. It is an unusual and highly specialized business designed to digest an advertiser's selling and marketing problems and produce ideas that will increase his sales, his reputation, and his profits. It's a good business, when it's run right, and makes good money for those who operate it. This book is intended as a working tool to help agency management run their businesses right.

Advertising is at the same time both big business and small business. In 1985 some $95.1 billion were spent on advertising in the United States—surely a vital force in the American economy and big business by any standard. About 42 percent of this, or approximately $40 billion, was spent through advertising agencies; and yet about 80 percent of this merely passed through the agencies on its way to media and suppliers, leaving the agencies with between $6 and $8 billion on which to operate, pay their people, and earn a profit. The biggest agencies reported their gross income from U. S. operations to be about $340 million—which is not big business by American standards.

Adding to the confusion is the fact that the term "advertising agency" is often used very loosely. For instance, the latest available Census of Service Industries shows 9,668 advertising agencies which had payroll while the *Standard Directory of Advertising Agencies* currently lists only 3,562 agencies which operate 4,889 offices in the Unites States. On the local level, in Phoenix, Arizona, the telephone book lists 276 advertising agencies (of which only 15 are shown as belonging to the American Association of Advertising Agencies), the Census lists only 63, and the Standard Directory lists just 40 agency offices. In its 1986 tabulation of agency gross income and other data, *Advertising Age* listed 526 agencies.

In terms of number of employees in the United States, *Advertising Age* found that the largest had some 4,600 and the smallest only 2. The average was 129. Using money as the criterion of size, 35.4 percent of the agencies listed in 1985 reported gross income of less than $1.5 million while 57.7 percent reported less than $3 million.

So, it seems accurate to say that advertising is a big business and an important factor in the American economy that is conducted by a large number of small business enterprises. It is for these enterprises, and for people who are thinking about getting into the business, that this book has been written.

In its original form in 1964, the book was basically a compilation and amplification of the various "Agencies Ask Us" columns written by Kenneth Groesbeck for *Advertising Age* over a period of years. It expressed a philosophy of agency operations that is still valid and that has been retained in the current revision.

In revising and enlarging this book, the material has been reorganized and grouped into sections covering financial operations, ownership, and internal organization. The original material has been revised, as needed, to reflect current agency operations and has been expanded to incorporate knowledge gained in a 45-year career in agency administration and finance. It is not intended that this book make the reader an advertising man, but rather, that it make him an advertising businessman.

Herbert S. Gardner, Jr.

I Advertising Agency Fundamentals

1
The Philosophy of Success

What does it take to bring success to an advertising agency? Certainly an agency must have sound procedures, a reasonable amount of billing, and adequate financial resources. Without them no business can succeed.

The necessary additional ingredient is a basic philosophy of business encompassing the two attributes that enable an agency to grow and prosper. These are *attitude* and *ability*. Neither by itself is sufficient. Both are needed and of the two, a proper attitude is much rarer.

What It Takes to Succeed

It is important for a young agency to realize that it cannot hold and build business just by copywriting ability, good art work, or even ingenuity in promotional ideas, however good they are. All these abilities are important, but they are not fundamental. Without basic soundness in selling judgment, they amount to nothing but fireworks with which to please and impress the client, and clients have an unpleasant habit of waking up from these dreams of greatness. Cleverness and ingenuity are a dime a dozen in our business and are often confused with ability. Actually, ability should enable the young agency operator to see these talents in their proper light, as a means rather than an end. Ability should give him good business judgment about his own operation, as well as those he endeavors to guide. Finally, real ability will dictate a proper attitude to the agency operator.

And what is this proper attitude? Well, for want of a better term, let's call it professionalism.

Just as a physician's whole aim is to cure a patient or better yet, by proper preventive care keep the illness from occurring in the first place, an agency's aim should be to improve the client's position and swell his profits by increasing sales, decreasing costs, or a combination of the two.

The agency must be in a position to give its client good business advice and to do so *it must know more about advertising than its client does*. Besides that, the agency must wholeheartedly believe in its knowledge and expertise, and must demonstrate that belief by the sincerity with which it presents recommendations to its client. This requires tact, diplomacy, and knowledge of human nature. If you plunge ahead blindly and insist that the client do something your way just because you say so, you can quickly lose the business. Remember always that you are dealing with areas of knowledge in which much uncertainty exists, proofs are difficult, and results stem from multiple causes. If, however, your attitude clearly shows that the betterment of the client's business is your sole purpose, at least you will be talking his or her own language. This factor alone should put you in a position in which your promotional advice is carefully considered.

Contrast this with the attitude of most young agencies: their primary end is to please the client. They make their plans and they write their copy in the hope of receiving the client's approval. Such agencies are unwittingly proceeding on the assumption that the client knows more about advertising than they do, which completely wipes out the reason for the agency's existence, apart from its mechanical functions.

Of course, we all know why so many agencies occupy this nonprofessional and subservient position in the economic scheme. Primarily it is because the results of advertising are so far removed from its creation and are further confused by the impact of other forces. So a client, concerned with the practical problems of sales and experienced in promotion, may well feel he or she knows as much or more about advertising than the agency. Occasionally he or she is right. So it is quite natural for the young agency to yield in such a situation, abandoning its birthright, if you please, and giving the client whatever he or she wants.

Taking the easiest way out, however, can be fatal to the agency. Sooner or later another agency will come along prepared to provide a better professional attitude and equipped to give the client what the present agency has failed to offer. The account predictably changes hands.

One more important point about attitude. Agencies must recognize themselves for what they are — experts capable of using sound professional advice to improve the client's results — and that their service is an immensely valuable one for which they are entitled to adequate remuneration. Worthwhile advertisers will respect you more for demanding what you are worth, and brother, unless you do, you are in for trouble.

So, by way of summary: for an agency to grow and prosper it must have a business philosophy combining both ability and attitude which demonstrate that it is capable of offering its clients sound business advice, that it is willing to rely on its own professionalism in doing so, and that it has the courage to charge what its advice is worth.

The Mystique of Growth

Should small agencies go along with the current trend to larger shops?

To adopt the title of a Gershwin song, "T'aint Necessarily So," it all depends on what you want. I know of many small agencies that do a thoroughly competent job for their clients and at the same time provide a satisfactory living for their owners and employees — and all of it far from the benzedrine and black coffee atmosphere so prevalent on Madison and Michigan Avenues. As the owner of one of these agencies put it: "I don't want growth in billings; I want growth in profits." So, in making its plans, the first thing an advertising agency should do is decide what it is shooting for. It may be set up only to make as much money as possible and grow as rapidly as it can. In this case, it must deliberately abandon many of the ambitions and ideals that concern agency heads. You can't concentrate on deals and high finance and have any time left to worry about increasing the sales and profits of your clients. And you can't carry water on both shoulders. Either you are set up to be a personal and conscientious adviser to some advertisers who trust you with their money, or you are only using this trust to advance yourself. In the long run, it will be found that not only is the agency business poorly suited for making a fast buck, but improper utilization of trust is very bad medicine indeed.

Let's concentrate on the small agency that mainly concerns itself with the excellence of its personal service to its clients, rather than with spectacular growth, and looks only for the growth that comes from growing with its clients.

To Grow You Must First Survive

In spite of the difficulty of operating in an era of increasing costs, small agencies are continually being born, keep on operating, and grow steadily, to a point where they provide a decent living for their people.

These successful agencies seem to conform to a common pattern. Externally, in the agency's relations with the outside world, it is a three-part pattern consisting of selling, planning, and performing; internally, within the agency's own management, it is good housekeeping combined with proper human relations. Let's look at each of these features in turn.

Selling. Smart small agencies find advertisers who need them. They make contact with these potential clients by letter, by telephone, then later with personal calls. They land a reasonable percentage of these prospects because they have what the advertiser needs, and they have developed ways of proving this in each case.

Planning.   Once the account is in the shop (and often even earlier, while the solicitation is proceeding), these good small agencies formulate, visualize, and present carefully worked-out programs for increasing the client's sales, profits, and company reputation. Part of the agency's planning must concern itself with the remuneration for its work and the division of labor between its staff and the client's sales staff, in what should be a joint effort to improve the client's situation. This frank facing of what may become an embarrassing business if delayed too long is extremely important. No agency can do a good job for a client if it is not getting enough money for its work. Successful agencies see in advance matters that later may cause misunderstanding and irritation on either side of the desk. Good planning includes complete listings of who does what and how much he is going to get for doing it.

Performance.   Agencies promise plenty in advance, in their selling and in their planning; good agencies' performances exceed their promises. Well, shouldn't they, after all? Previously, an agency was on the outside looking in, handicapped by a lack of knowledge of the real difficulties confronting the advertiser. Now it is on the inside. It is a member of the client's family. In a well-organized relationship, nothing important is hidden from the agency. Assuming the agency has what it takes, its staff brings wide experience and business judgment to bear upon problems which may have disconcerted an advertiser who has been up to his ears in them for years. New brains, new enthusiasm, new approaches, new results!

This personal attention, this identification of the client's welfare with that of the agency, is one of the cogent reasons for small agency success.

Good housekeeping.   This homely term best describes the successful internal management that marks the good small agency. Its financial affairs are sound. It gets paid what it deserves. It spends less than it takes in. It utilizes the resulting profit in three ways: working capital, frosting on the cake for the owners, and profit-sharing for the crew of the ship.

Proper human relations.   This is both an internal and an external attitude. The good agency behaves properly toward its clients and its suppliers. It is honest and decent in its dealings, reliable and careful with promises, and prodigal in performance. Also, the good agency is good to work for. It takes proper care of its people. It may pay them conservatively, since it plays its finances very safe, but whatever profits there are it shares liberally. There is no feeling that the boss gets all the gravy or all the credit for ideas. Every person in the agency is happier working in that shop than he or she would be working for him- or herself.

Bulwarks Against Hard Times

The margin on which an ad agency operates is very slim. It takes very little reduction in income or increase in expenses to turn a profit into a loss. Also, because it's so highly visible, the advertising budget frequently is, unfortunately, one of the first places cut when the client begins to feel the pinch. So another vital part of the pattern for survival is the adoption of policies that will build bulwarks to protect the agency against temporary setbacks. Here are three such bulwarks,

Cash money.   Agencies strong enough to weather bad times have built up their working capital steadily in years of prosperity instead of spending on larger quarters, unnecessary improvements, and too-generous profit sharing. It is a good rule to plow back a substantial part of their profits into the business, although such sums are subject to federal taxes. Where working capital has been small in relation to needs, many agencies have reinvested in themselves higher than normal percentages of their good time profits, aiming at an eventual working capital figure large enough not only to handle all normal needs such as earning cash discounts and establishing excellent credit, but also to provide the extra margin of safety desirable for any business. A good rule of thumb is to build your working capital until it equals about one quarter of your total annual payroll. This will give you a cushion so you don't have to cut salaries and people at the first sign of a loss of billing, and thus throw overboard your most valuable asset—your people and their morale.

Multiple ownership.   The strongest agencies are those in which valuable people have been allowed to become part owners of the agency. Profit sharing is fine, but real ownership is better. Too many agencies, built up by the ability of the founder, strive to maintain this benevolent autocracy.

A word of warning must be sounded in connection with this principle. In choosing people to participate in ownership, first be sure of the real value of the individuals concerned. Go slowly and surely, and give yourself an escape hatch in case the person concerned does not live up to expectations.

Diversification of accounts.   In seeking new business, agencies should be wary of big accounts that may take all the agency's resources and abilities. The later loss of such business could almost wreck an agency. No one would be so foolish as to advise passing up a big account if you can get it, but at the same time be aware of the dangers inherent in dependence upon income from one single source. Go after many small accounts as well; take them on fees if necessary. Don't lose money on any one of them. Take bread and butter accounts, and industrial accounts. They're less glamorous, perhaps, but safe and sure, and appreciate the attention other agencies have denied them. Diversify. This policy has paid off richly for agencies in surviving difficult times.

These, then, are three basic policies which have helped agencies weather temporary reversals. They concern, as you see, money, people, and new business. They exemplify wise business judgment in how to cope not only with normal bad breaks, but also with the particular hazards which characterize the agency business.

So Having Survived, How About Growth?

By far your best source of new business is your present list of clients. Why? Well, in the first place, because you know them and they know you; then, they have confidence in you or they'd be your ex-clients instead of your clients; you're helping them grow and as they continue to grow so will you. But, you can't just sit back and take this for granted; you must keep continually reminding the client how valuable you are to him or her. Here are some specific things you should do.

First, do outstandingly good, creative work. By that I mean new and advanced marketing ideas expressed in excellent copy, ingenious and effective point-of-sale material, and constant cooperation with the sales department of the advertiser.

Second, rub the advertiser's nose in this good work, tactfully and persuasively. If you don't tell him, and if possible prove to him how good and effective the advertising is, he may not realize it. He doesn't know about advertising. How do you expect him to do it justice unless you constantly sell it to him and the sales force?

Third, make the advertiser realize how much he is getting for his money. Contact reports help in this, but examples of money saving, space or time bought on better terms, production costs held down by skillful repetition of advertisements, and competitive prices from vendors—all these the agency should forcefully call to the advertiser's attention. It isn't enough to do an able job in landing his account. You have to keep on selling it as long as it is in the shop.

Fourth, remember that ours is a personal service business. The more you can keep all your client contacts on a highly personal and friendly basis, the more you can identify yourself with his or her business, the better off you will be. The small agency principals can afford to give more time to individual clients. They have time to worry, which is important. This situation accounts for the many agency-client relationships which are so long-lasting, and which are usually terminated only by change in the personnel of the agency or the advertiser.

Fifth, although you may not be able to afford extra departments and services, you must offer them and make it constantly clear that whatever the advertiser could get from larger agencies he can get from you. It probably will be necessary to buy such services on the outside; however, the client needs to be told they are available. Remember, other agencies are constantly telling him how much he is missing.

Always remember that, in spite of whatever is done to get better and bigger, there will be a normal mortality rate among accounts, through no fault of yours. This attrition must be provided for in advance by constantly gunning for new business, in part to replace what will be lost, in part to continue growth.

No agency stands still. It either gains or loses. The agency that appears to be running along on an even keel with about the same billing every year is actually losing ground. Time is running out on it. The longer it holds on to an account, doing much the same thing year after year, the more the advertiser wonders if he wouldn't possibly do better elsewhere. Sadly enough, our vulnerability increases with length of service. It's unfortunate, but there it is.

Every business has its good and its bad points. Ours is a remunerative, exciting, rewarding occupation. It is also highly unstable, subject to personal whims and vagaries, little understood by the man who pays the bills.

You've got to be fast on your feet, sensitive to unexpected developments, able to smell smoke a mile off, alway conscious of the advertiser's pulse rate, and aware of his attitude toward you before he senses it himself.

Yes, get better and get bigger as fast as is economically practicable. But most of all, get smarter. Learn how to think two jumps ahead of the client. Don't follow, lead. You're supposed to know more about promoting sales than he or she does; show that you do.

We tend to blame our losses of business on the larger size of other agencies, or on their offering something we cannot afford or should not offer. But are these the real reasons why another shop landed the business? We don't hold billing by being as good as our competitors; we hold it only by being better, and constantly proving it. Basically advertisers don't want to change agencies, in spite of their inherent restlessness. They know how much time will be required to educate the new agency. They'd like to stay, if we give them a reason by proving that it is to their best interest to stay put.

2

Some Economic Facts of Agency Life

Most agency principals are outgoing, creative people whose main motivation is to do a good job for the client. They instinctively dislike numbers that limit their freedom of action; however, knowing and understanding the lesser-known economic facts of agency life are vital to an agency's existence.

Some Pitfalls to Avoid

"What pitfalls must many agency people, particularly those who are contemplating forming their own agencies, avoid? What causes agencies to fail?"

When considering what you must watch out for—the rocks and shoals that can wreck even the best planned agency—you must always bear in mind the narrow margin on which the agency business operates. Based on figures from the American Association of Advertising Agencies, as published in *Advertising Age* from time to time, out of every dollar billed to the client, the agency immediately paid out to the media and suppliers just over 79 cents, leaving just over 20 cents to meet all its own expenses and earn a profit. Less than one cent remains as profit. Here are the figures:

	Client Dollars	Agency Dollars
Billed to Clients	$100.00	
Paid to Media & Suppliers	79.56	
Retained by Agency	20.44	$100.00
Agency's Expenses	19.34	94.60
Profit Before Taxes	1.10	5.40
Income Taxes	0.27	1.34
Net Profit	0.83	4.06

Runaway Expenses
The first pitfall is failure to watch expenses like a hawk. These figures show that an expenditure of $11.00 for a client lunch must generate an additional $1,000 of billing or profit will suffer. Pretty scary, isn't it?

Employee Attitudes
A closely related pitfall is the failure to impress all your employees, and especially the account executives, that while they are working on the *client's* account, they are working for the *agency*. Never let them forget that their paychecks come from the agency and not from the client.

Of course, the agency and all its people must do the best job they can for the client, but they must exercise good business judgment when doing so. All too often this is interpreted as giving the client everything he or she could possibly want, such as four or five versions of every layout or the regular acceptance of rush jobs entailing overtime work. True, these all have to be done at times, but the agency man or woman who is thinking of the agency's (and his or her own) welfare as well as the client's wishes will insist on billing the client for the extras involved. He or she will probably be suprised to learn that, if properly approached with logical reasoning, the client is a reasonable person, too. There will be times when you have to give away services like these, but if your people are properly instructed in good business practices, at least you'll know what you're giving away and why.

Lack of Planning
By their very nature, agencies are highly dependent on the talents of a small group of people—and in their early stages, on the talents of one man. So a prolonged illness or death can play havoc with an agency that hasn't foreseen these possibilities and made some advance provisions to meet them. Various kinds of insurance can help here, as well as plans for the succession of responsibilities in both the management of the agency and the handling of client contacts.

Poor Management
Generally this arises because of the nature of the typical advertising person: creative, imaginative, impulsive, and outgoing, but often without knowledge of finance. He works hard, does a grand creative and marketing job, gives more service than he can possibly afford, and comes to the year-end with a loss instead of a profit and the inescapable question, "How long can I stand this drain?" So, our agency principal must either acquire a sense for sound financial management or hire someone to manage the agency's

finances. Most simply defined, this means spending less than you take in, thus showing a profit.

Profit can be increased in only two ways—either by reducing expenses or by increasing income. To maintain such a policy day in and day out requires courage on the part of the agency principal—the courage to say no to many requests for increased salaries or other expenditures and the courage to ask clients for more income in the form of fees or other charges when expenses cannot be cut further.

Go Easy on Extending Credit

Except in a few cases, like advertising for political candidates, advertising is placed and paid for on credit, not cash. How far should an agency go in extending credit?

The imprudent extension of credit is undoubtedly the biggest pitfall of all. The peculiar economics of the agency business, with the agency working for the advertiser and yet being paid by the media through commissions, has its origins in the very early days when agencies were primarily brokers who bought space in wholesale quantities and re-sold it to their clients. Somewhere along the line they began to write copy to fill the space they had bought and the agency creative function was born. In those days, the media were dealing only with the agencies and obviously looked to them for payment for the space they bought. This is still a fundamental principle of the normal agency-media relationship and the contract form most commonly used states that, "Publisher agrees to hold Agency solely liable for payment."

In the aftermath of the Lennen & Newell and U.S. Media International failures, there was a definite trend to back away from agency sole liability, particularly on the part of the networks. In 1974, two networks sued advertisers for unpaid bills, but in 1977 the courts ruled against the networks, thus upholding the principle of sole agency responsibility for payment to media. This action apparently did not finally resolve the issue because CBS and Stokely-Van Camp reached an out-of-court settlement under which Stokely paid CBS a reputed $50,000 to save the cost of fighting the appeal which CBS had just filed. So, the question is still open as to how much liability falls on the advertiser.

In the meantime a minor cottage industry has sprung up that designs and sells insertion orders and similar forms containing a disclaimer clause whereby the agency seeks to protect itself against sole financial liability on the grounds that it is acting as a true agent for a disclosed principal (the client). As far as I know none of these has been tested legally and I would certainly urge an agency to consult its attorneys before adopting such disclaimer forms.

Some agencies are including in their contract forms a limited liability clause; a typical one states "Agency shall pay for . . . broadcasts carried by Station . . . only if it first receives payment . . . from its client." Whether or not this would hold up in court no one knows.

In any event, the whole question of agency liability for media payments is very much up in the air, particularly since a lot of broadcast advertising is run without any formal signed contract at all. This interchange between agency and station is all too common:

Agency: "Here's a contract and schedule for X spots."

Station: "Thanks for your order. Here's our confirming contract. Please sign and return it."

Agency: "We don't like this or that about your contract. Why not sign our form as confirmation?"

Station: "We can't do that because of - - - - - - -."

This dialogue can go on for so long that the spots involved probably have been run without a single piece of paper signed by agency or client.

So until the situation has been cleared up by the courts, the prudent agency principal had better assume that he is going to be held liable for payment to media. This means that his neck is on the line and he must use due care in extending credit to his clients. Unfortunately, clients seldom ask for credit extension in advance. They simply take it, a little more each month as the agency proves too much afraid of provoking the client and losing the account to complain loudly. Soon they are into it for ten, twenty, thirty thousand dollars, and the agency may be obligated to borrow from the bank to carry the debt and maintain its own credit with media and suppliers. A fine kettle of fish!

To avoid this dilemma, it is preferable not to extend credit at all. Set your billing dates and terms of payment so that you get your money before you're required to pay it out. Since this is contrary to the way most agencies operate, many feel that clients will resist the realistic request for payment before the agency is holding the bag. Not so! When the situation is properly presented, most honest clients see the reasonableness of the request, and think more highly of the agency that pursues this policy.

But—and this is very important—put your method and timing of billing in writing and discuss it frankly with the client as early in your relationship with him as possible. Also, be sure at this point to get the client's financial men in on the act. They'll know what you're talking about and see the reasonableness of your arguments. Point out that, if they don't pay promptly, you're putting $79 of your own on the line in the expectation of keeping 83 cents. They'll get the idea!

Another point. Watch your receivables as though your life depended on it—for your corporate life may. Start to scream bloody murder the minute a bill becomes overdue. There's no surer recipe for the bankruptcy of an agency than to pay media for space or time you ordered and then have your client renege on paying you. By all means look into credit insurance; it can be expensive, particularly for less than top-rated clients, but it just may save your neck.

One last thought on the subject of credit. This is the matter of recognition which is granted by individual media or in many cases by such organizations as Media Credit Association (MCA) acting on behalf of many media. Recognition is simply a certification, based on an examination of your financial statements, that you seem to be financially reliable and can be expected to discount your bills. New statements are requested every six months or year to keep up to date. Formerly an agency without recognition was denied the 15 percent commission but the only penalty today is a denial of credit and a requirement to pay cash with your order.

Just as the media keep an eye constantly on the agency through the recognition procedure, so the agency should keep an eye on its clients' financial health.

Subscribe to a regular financial reporting service such as Dun & Bradstreet. Don't take the attitude that this implies any distrust of your clients. It's just good business practice when you may be extending to a single client over the course of a year credit in an amount that exceeds your total working capital. To paraphrase Andrew Carnegie, you have all your eggs in one basket—so for Heaven's sake watch that basket closely.

Don't Finance Your Clients

Should an agency finance its clients? What does this really mean? What's so bad about it?

It always has been considered one of the cardinal principles of the agency business that the agency is expected to finance its own operations, but not the advertising of its clients.

The first part of this statement simply means that the principals of an agency should be good enough businessmen to operate at a profit and thus avoid dissipating the agency's resources simply to stay afloat. It also means that the agency will have started with (or built up over the years with retained profits) enough capital to see it through the ordinary ups and downs of business.

This is not to say that an agency's own resources must be enough to meet any contingency, but that its past performance plus current resources should be enough so that it can get needed financing from regular commercial sources to tide it over an unusually severe short-term financial bind. The key phrase here is "commercial sources." Avoid like the plague seeking financial help from clients! This is the road that leads to becoming a "house agency" (dirty word), and ultimate loss of freedom of action and true professionalism.

Let's look now at agency financing of clients. This is usually more subtle and occurs whenever the agency extends longer than normal credit to the client. The case where an agency simply lets its client's bills run along unpaid has been discussed in the preceding section. A more common form of client financing arises from the way agencies handle payment for mechanical (and to a lesser extent broadcast) production.

Many jobs of this sort—particularly large catalogs and similar pieces— are in process for several weeks or even months before they are completed. As each particular supplier involved in the job finishes his work he'll send in his bill and the well-managed agency will pay it within its terms. If, however, the agency's billing arrangements with its clients call for billing production only when the job has been completed, it cannot rebill to the client the amount it has paid out to the supplier, but must put it into a suspense account called "inventory" or "work in process" or some similar term. To the extent that such an account remains on the books, it constitutes financing the client's advertising. There are ways to get around this; they'll be covered in chapter 9, "Billing for Your Services."

The ultimate example of financing the client occurs when the client has owed the agency money for a long time and professes inability to pay in cash, but offers his company's stock instead. Don't even think twice about it; utter a resounding "No!" Chances are, you'd probably lose your shirt, or at least a good part of it, and at best would be stuck with a frozen asset or questionable value.

If you have to accept something other than cash for your bills, get an interest-bearing note with a fixed maturity. If you have to, you can probably discount this at the bank. A corollary benefit of doing this is that in some cases, merely asking for a promissary note has resulted in payment of the debt in full, in cash.

This is not to say that you should never own a client's stock. The situation just described should not be confused with the situation in which an agency desires voluntarily to invest in its client's business, believing that its inside track puts it in a position to make a desirable profit by getting in on the ground floor of a situation not yet spotted by other investors. That's the way many advertising pioneers became rich.

So why shouldn't an agency finance a client?

Basically because it's not in the financing business (that's what banks are for); it has no skills in providing financing nor the investigatory facilities to tell a good financing deal from a bad one; and it has no mechanism set up to handle the details involved in financing. You're much better off to stick to your knitting—to what you know best.

Beware of Cut-rating, Rebating, Speculating

Another common problem is that there are many agencies that practice a kick-back system in secret. Should you plan to swap punches with them *sub rosa?* Should you admit the situation and compete openly on a price basis? Also, what about speculative presentations?

This may seem like a mixed up group of unrelated questions, but in reality they are quite similar and the answers to them will go far toward establishing your basic economic philosophy. How you answer will show how strongly you believe the old maxim that the worker is worth his hire.

Don't for a minute forget that the only things you or any agency have to sell are the time and talents of yourself and your associates. If you regularly give them away below their real worth, clients and prospective clients can't be blamed for accepting your evaluation. And you'll have trouble generating enough income to stay in business, let alone grow and prosper. Have the courage of your convictions and charge what your services are worth. The client will respect you for it.

While there is nothing wrong about an agency cutting prices to get new business, these questions pose another aspect of the problem, that is, does it work? It often gets business. But then what?

All too frequently an agency that gets a piece of new business by price cutting gives the impression that this is its normal operating procedure and the client comes to expect all future work to be on the same low cost basis. Agency service, for the best interests of the advertiser, consists of hard thinking and planning to increase the client's sales, reputation, and profits. This means time spent by the agency heads and the top talent, not the clerical force or any other of the mechanical elements of the agency operation. An agency simply cannot afford to use this expensive talent to the extent it should, unless it is liberally paid for it. With competition what it is, nothing but the best has a chance to be seen and to be effective. The best costs money. No agency can hope to live and increase, to make a profit year after year, to grow in strength and reputation, if large portions of its business are regularly handled on the basis of price concessions.

What about the client who asks to be billed at less than the standard markup or to have part of the normal commission rebated to him?

First, there is nothing really wrong with this practice, but for years it was considered anathema and all kinds of subterfuges were used to avoid even the appearance of rebating.

I know of one completely reputable advertiser who was billed for broadcast talent with a mark up or only 5% by his equally reputable agency; another agency paid for a lot of research studies made for the benefit of a specific client. In both instances the agency and its client were adjusting the agency's income in one case and its costs in the other so that it would earn a reasonable profit on its total effort for the client.

Just as an agency can't grow and prosper by regularly undercharging for its services, neither can it do so by regularly overcharging the client and making inordinate profits. Both of the instances cited above were deliberate afforts jointly undertaken by agency and client to make sure that the agency was making what both agreed was a reasonable profit. Obviously this kind of arrangement required, and received, review by both parties at frequent intervals to reflect changing conditions.

Finally, what about speculative presentations? Aside from being expensive and of questionable value, they can present real dangers to the agency. Probably the greatest of these is that the agency may inadvertently put itself in a bad light. Without knowing much more about the prospect's business, aims, and problems than any agency could possibly know without working closely with the advertiser, the speculative work may be completely off target.

How much better for the agency to say, "We don't know enough about your business to design an intelligent campaign, but here are some examples of successful campaigns we have designed for clients with whom we have worked long enough to understand their business thoroughly." Then parade some of your best work, adding comments on the problem to be solved. In fact, one agency regularly refers to such exhibits not as "examples of our work" but rather as "solutions to problems."

Another danger, though one frequently more imagined than real, is that a prospect may not give the account to the agency making the speculative presentation, but would appropriate for its own use the ideas or materials submitted. There are several ways to prevent this problem from occurring. One agency principal always puts a date on every such piece to show clearly that it originated before the presentation; another always clearly indicates on the materials that they belong to the agency. Probably the surest way to handle the problem is to refuse to present speculative material to a prospect you think is capable of stealing it. Of course, if the prospect reimburses the agency for the speculative material the question of plagiarism doesn't arise because, having paid for it, the advertiser owns the material.

On balance, I urge agencies to avoid speculative presentations in all but the most unusual circumstances, and even then, to try to get the advertiser to pick up the tab.

Thus, to summarize this whole subject of competing on the basis of price, I would urge any agency to stick to its guns and consistently charge what its services are worth. If your costs are actually lower, so you can charge less without diluting your profit, by all means take advantage of this true competitive edge. But don't sell yourself short. While this may pick up some billing on the short term, it will be self-defeating in the long run.

3

Getting Started in the Agency Business

When I talk about getting into the agency business, I am talking about getting to the point where you are the principal owner of an agency (or at least one of a small number of principals). You can reach this point by going to work as an employee of an establishd agency and gradually buying stock as it becomes available, but this book is not concerned with this usually slow process. Instead it is considering how you go about starting your own agency or buying an existing one and thus becoming, as it were, an instant owner.

Should You Start Your Own Agency?

Hope must indeed still spring eternal and the entrepreneurial urge run strong judging by the number of inquiries I've had about going into the agency business.

Some optimists think it looks like an easy way to make money and just want to be told how to go about it. Other better qualified businessmen, with genuine reasons for starting their own shops, ask to have their figures checked out. Here are a few observations that may by useful.

First of all, remember that most people who plan on going into the agency business underestimate their expenses and overestimate their income, so it is wise to allow a large margin of error to compensate for this natural human attitude. Be conservative in your original planning to avoid rude shocks later on.

An advertising agency is an expensive operation, involving a place in which to work, furniture, fixtures, and equipment. A number of people must be hired, according to the volume of business you plan to handle at the outset.

These expenses will be of two sorts, initial (non-recurring) and continuous (operating). The funds to meet initial expenses must come from the original capital advanced by the founders.

Once the agency is set up and ready for business the question becomes "Where is the money coming from for operating expenses, and how soon?"The second part of this question is important. There is a lag, often of many weeks, between the time an agency incurs a financial obligation or actually has to pay out money, and the time when cash is received from the client.

The first thing to look at, then, is gross income for the agency. This means the money the agency retains after paying media and suppliers and which it uses to pay expenses. To the greatest possible degree, this gross income must be sure. It must be adequate. Lacking either of these characteristics, you are headed for trouble.

Therefore, start out by investigating the realistic expectation of continuing income. This is not easy because, even if you have written assurances from clients based on their advertising plans, there is nothing to prevent these plans from being changed or delayed. If you can get a contract involving fees you are better off, but this may be hard for a new agency.

Not only must you get business in order to run an agency—you must make sure you will be able to hold on to it. Most contracts give you only 90 days protection. Theoretically your entire business, and the income derived from it, can fly out the window within this time. To retain advertising or promotional billings, you must continuously deliver satisfactory service. That, in turn, depends entirely on people—yourself and your associates.

So there is a clear element of risk involved in the question of income to the agency. It is difficult to figure this risk correctly; however, your success or failure may rest squarely on how you solve this problem.

So, having assured a continuing income, as best you can, the question becomes, "How much income is necessary?" All the current figures show that income should be at least 20 percent of billing—so an agency billing a nice round $5 million should try to get gross income of $1 million, at the least. Since media commissions are at a fixed rate of 15 percent of billing, the difference will have to come from markups on outside purchases, charges for copy, art, etc. done by your own people and, quite likely, fees of one sort or another. You must be prepared to draw up a schedule of charges for these services. It must be competitive in your market; it must be one you can justify to clients; and, above all, it must produce the income you need to reach your $1 million.

You also must be prepared to operate, initially, at a loss. Even if you budget your expenses so they will absorb only $900,000 of your $1 million on a regular basis, and thus give you a 10 percent profit, you will be in the red for quite a while initially. This results from the lag between the time the idea is born, the client is billed, and you are paid. A reasonable allowance for this is three months.

So, an agency just starting business will begin incurring expenses, for salaries, rent, etc., the day it opens its doors, but will not receive any appreciable income (except from fees) for about three months. In this period it will have spent one quarter of its annual expense budget or, using our sample figures, $225,000. It would be in the hole by the difference between that figure and the incidental income and fees received. Obviously, it is going to take a while to start showing a profit.

This points up another factor the new agency head must consider: the necessity of providing enough capital to buy needed furniture, typewriters, etc., and to cover operating expenses until income really starts coming in. A good rule of thumb for an agency of the size described here would be $250,000 or 25 percent of anticipated annual gross income. If you can't put up that much yourself, or borrow it, you can consider offering part ownership to some of the key people who will be working with you, but don't do this unless you know them and their abilities thoroughly. Above all, during your starting days don't allow any outsider to make even a small investment of cash in your enterprise just to build up your working capital. When you do this, you are selling part of your business before you know what it is worth and before you know as much as you should about the person involved. This, I find, is a mistake made frequently by people new to the agency business. It can be embarrassing and expensive.

Once the new agency is assured of income and its continuance, the next requirement for success would seem to be knowing where you are at all times. How you are doing, month by month. This, of course, calls for experienced financial management.

You will best allocate this job to someone else, since it is difficult, specialized work and you are likely to need all your time running your shop and keeping both your clients and your people happy. You will need an accurate cost system, administered by an expert. Don't economize on this. It can make or break you. You must be apprised steadily of whether you are running ahead or behind, where you are making money, and where you are losing. Given this information, you must act on it fast and with courage, allowing yourself to be influenced as little as possible by emotion.

Finally, I would suggest as an essential of success in today's business that you sense your client's needs before he does. Don't sit back comfortably assuming that everything is all right just because the relationship is continuing and nobody seems to be complaining. Your security is constantly being undermined by the client's normal dissatisfaction with everything except his own performance, and by claims set up by competing agencies. I strongly believe that the future of the entire agency business, and getting proper payment for its work, depends upon the extent to which agencies render valuable business advice.

So, by way of summary and with a note of encouragement, you've set up an agency, assured a reasonable and continuing income, and weathered the first rough months. Now, how do you earn a profit, and having earned it, what do you do with it?

You turn a profit in managing an agency by first setting the profit aside, then running the business by spending only what's left over. It's like managing a household budget by putting a series of coffee cans labeled "groceries," "clothes," "rent," "insurance," etc. on a shelf. At the beginning of each month, you divide up the money for running the household and put the proper amount in each of the coffee cans. When a payment is to be made, you take the money out of the appropriate can—but never out of the neighboring one.

In your case as agency manager, one of your cans is labeled "profit." (In actual practice this "can" might be a special bank account.) Whenever a dollar of gross income is received you immediately take 20 cents of it (or whatever amount represents your planned profit) and put it in the profit can. Only after you've done this do you divide the remainder of the gross income among the other cans which represent different kinds of operating expenses. Like the household manager who scrupulously respects the can labels, never take anything out of the profit can until the end of the year. Then you divide up the contents between bonuses, profit sharing, additions to working capital, etc.—all, of course, according to plan.

You show a profit from an advertising agency only if you decide to operate so a profit is assured, which means sacrifice and rigid economy. Some people are content to operate only for their own pay and that of those associated with them, in the hope of future growth. This is unwise. Insisting on a profit is more than a theoretical desirability; it makes for financial soundness and assures capital growth. It definitely bears on the agency's credit position.

In the early days of the agency you may feel that paying part of your profits to your employees in the form of profit sharing is premature, in which event you split your profits between yourself and your business in whatever proportions seem best. However, the sooner your associates begin sharing in the shop's profits, the sounder your personnel relations will be.

Should You Buy an Agency?

Instead of going through the problems of starting a new agency, wouldn't it be better to buy one already operating? If so, what should you look out for? On its face this seems like a good idea—if you are buying what you think you are, if the values are really there, and if the price is right. For the moment let's forget about price, which is covered in the valuation section of chapter 11, and talk about what you're buying.

You're Buying Net Assets

This is pretty simple and the main thing to check out is that the assets are real and not imaginary, and that all offsetting liabilities, both present and contingent, are disclosed. Accounts receivable from clients are usually one of the largest assets and one of the hardest to evaluate properly. They should be examined critically to see if there are substantial amounts that are in dispute or badly in arrears — and adjustments made accordingly. All of this is the kind of thing any competent accountant with some knowledge of agencies can evaluate and you certainly should hire one to do so.

You're Buying Future Earning Power

This has been called "going business value" or "goodwill" but, in its simplest terms, you are buying a source of future income and the facilities to handle that income and convert it into continuing profits. There are several major components of this future earning power.

Clients.   The continuing loyalty of clients is the lifeblood of the agency business. Have the important clients been taken into anybody's confidence and told about the impending sale of the agency? Or have they just been left in the dark for fear that consulting them might rock the boat? "Rock" is a mild term for it when they are offered, as a *fait accompli*, a brand new agency picture they may or may not like.

Barring actual guarantees of continuance by responsible clients, account shifts are more likely than not, especially when new agency personnel are involved. New ownership gives the client an "out" if he has been looking for one. His obligations to past ownership are now discharged. He fears a chance of agency policy, so "it's a good time to be looking around to see if we can buy anything better, or for less money." A very dangerous time, indeed.

People.   When you buy a conjectural future earning power, you must pay particular attention to the factors that will affect account retention. Possibly the most important of these is the personality of the agency owner and the account men who have been contacting and handling the business. Accounts stay with agencies, and correspondingly leave them, on a personal basis more often than is generally realized. We like to think accounts stay with us because of the good job we do for them; frequently, however, what holds them is the client's liking for the account executive.

So, buying an agency in which the previous owner and his key people stay on the job, is a very different proposition from buying one where they disappear from the picture. Good as the new owners may be, they are likely to be disagreeably disappointed by the way some business departs with their predecessors. So, assure yourself as much as possible of the continuing participation of the key people from the old regime.

Deals.   A stable list of clients is very important. But, behind that stability, are they all what they seem to be? Are there any special deals of one sort or another that would tend to make future income less than you'd expect? Better check them out!

Reputation.   When you take over as new owner you'll find your road a lot smoother if you have the support and backing of the local media, suppliers, banks, civic organizations, etc. It'll be a lot easier to get and keep this support if the agency you're taking over has a good reputation in town. Check it out. Tell these groups of your plans and enlist their support. It should be easy to get if you start from a good base.

So, having determined what you're buying, it's wise to stop a minute and look with a jaundiced eye at why the agency is for sale. If it's as sound and profitable as it appears, why does the present owner want out? Maybe he is just getting tired of the rat race and wants to take things easy; maybe family health dictates a better climate; or just maybe (how cynical can you get?) he knows something and is trying to unload a potential lemon. Take a while to look into this gift horse's mouth—it may save you a bundle of bucks.

Since, as Robert Burns so aptly said, "The best laid plans of mice and men gang aft a-gley," try to provide an escape hatch in case things really go sour. Of course, if an agreement has been entered into in good faith, the honorable purchaser will be bound by its terms even if the business falls apart completely. But the terms of payment or the basis for calculating the final total price can be so drawn as to provide some relief in case of a serious reverse. It's far better to think of all the bad things that can happen and try to provide for them in advance, in a calm and reasoned way, than to try to devise emergency measures in the midst of a crisis.

4

To Thine Own Self
Be True

Advertising can take many forms—one woman telling another about a product she likes (word-of-mouth, the best there is); a million dollars' worth of time and talent over a nationwide television network; a card saying "good for colds" on your druggist's counter; a postcard from your car dealer; a turtle with "Souvenir of Miami" painted on its shell; a four-color gatefold in a national magazine; the smell of popcorn coming out of a store window.

All these are advertising, and if you try to say what they have in common you will come up with two correct conclusions: they are all forms of communication and they all aim to convince someone of something.

It has been said frequently that the aim of advertising is the sale. This, however, is true only in some cases. Such forms of advertising as mail order and direct mail aim almost solely to complete the sale. By far the greatest volume of advertising, however, aims at conviction only, the establishment of a favorable frame of mind, so that when the demand and the supply source come together, the sale results.

Advertising prepares the ground. It informs and convinces the consumer initially that a product or service is desirable and then that a specific product or service fits that desirable image.

This situation is true of the majority of products and services we use and of general ideas we entertain. For almost everything there is in our minds a picture or an image, concerning which we subconsciously feel: "This is what it should be."

An agency's main reason for existence is its ability to give good promotional advice. It offers experienced business judgment in the narrow and specialized field of selling. Once this good sense is utilized by the client for plans and strategies, it is further implemented by all the agency's copy and art talent, all its marketing know-how, and all its experience in buying space, time, and materials. It is most important for us to recognize this sequence, this double importance of plan and performance. Good strategy and smart execution are as good a formula as you are likely to encounter for advertising success.

Once you recognize the importance of this preliminary thinking—business judgment projected into the future—you see more clearly how important it is that the agency be free to speak its mind, influenced only by the best interests of the client. Anything that interferes with this free thinking and free speaking does the client a disservice.

What kinds of restrictions are there on an agency's freedom? There are several, and unfortunately they seem to be increasing in number and severity.

Fear of the Client

More than most of us are willing to admit, our recommendations are influenced by fear of the client. We make plans based on what we think the customer will approve, rather than what we know is best. This bad basic situation must be resisted at all times. Once we allow this expediency to govern us, we lose all standing as independent advisers. We have bowed to a conflict of interest. We have put immediate profits first. Any client who has sense enough to make a success of his own business quickly sizes us up correctly, and begins to look around, like Diogenes, for an honest agency.

Another aspect of this can arise as a result of the way an agency is compensated. If compensation is based primarily on the commission method, there may be an unconscious predilection on the agency's part to recommend increased media expenditures since this increases agency income, or there may be some feeling by the client that this is what the agency is doing.

If, on the other hand, the agency is compensated by fees, it can make whatever recommendations it sincerely feels are best for the client without in any way affecting its own income. I know of several cases in which agencies, under these circumstances, have recommended a cessation of all advertising for a period. This is real freedom to give sound advice.

False and Deceptive Advertising

As we all know, there is a dangerous and rapidly widening gap between consumers and producers of goods and services. There is increasing public distrust, not only of advertising, but of all business. How come? Well, by its very nature, advertising always operates in the full glare of publicity. So the errors, exaggerations, and downright falsehoods of the few, the rigged quiz shows on television, and the phony demonstrations are magnified and blown up to frightening proportions by publicity, scandal, and the well-recognized human propensity to find bad things more interesting than good ones.

Does this unfavorable opinion of advertising do the business real harm? Of course it does. Each piece of deception, major or minor, increases the incredulity defensive minds raise against all selling endeavors. The more advertising indicates to people that it cannot be trusted, the more it costs advertisers to create belief. Heaven knows there is enough normal resistance, without so stupidly increasing it!

Two attitudes characterize the buying frame of mind. One is a desire that the seller tell his story as favorably as possible, emphasizing its good points and minimizing its bad ones. So we find the buyer considering advertising a pleasing combination of all those devices the seller selects to please, attract attention, entertain, and create a favorable atmosphere. What a delightful prospect!

Alongside this friendly attitude, however, is another and sometimes even stronger attitude which may seem to be inconsistent. This is, "Don't fool me. You're signing your name to this story you're telling me. Lord help you if it isn't true!" Here is incipient resentment. And the more courteously a consumer has listened to your story, the madder he gets when he finds out he's been had.

The most hopeful element in the problem is the demonstrable fact that true, sincere, and informative advertising pays off, while false advertising falls flat on its face. So, regardless of restrictions imposed by outside sources, the pure economics of advertising dictate that the wise agency, in its own selfish interests, should put restrictions on its freedom of action. It should strive to produce only sincere, honest, and informative advertising.

Industry Self-Regulation

Another limitation on agency freedom is found in the advertising industry's own regulatory mechanism. This takes many different forms, some of them of long standing.

Individual Media

The earliest example of self-regulation was the establishment of standards by individual publishers or broadcasters. These usually have taken the form of an "advertising acceptability guide," but two prominent magazines, *Good*

Housekeeping and *Parents,* have adopted seals of approval which they grant to advertisers whose products pass strict performance tests and meet their advertised claims. Since each of these sets of standards is different, you may find yourself with an advertisement that is acceptable to one medium, but not to another. A good example is the major oil company which had a commercial rejected as controversial by two television networks, yet completely accepted by the third.

Industry Groups

As early as 1924 the American Association of Advertising Agencies (AAAA) drew up a creative code setting forth standards of ethics and good taste in advertising. This code now has been endorsed by almost all major advertising and advertiser associations.

The first major effort to set up a mandatory code came in 1952 when the National Association of Broadcasters (NAB) drew up a code for both radio and television which set forth standards of good taste and acceptability for both commercials and program content.

In 1971 the National Advertising Review Board (NARB) was set up with the support of all sectors of the advertising industry. Its pupose is to deal effectively with deception and bad taste in national advertising. As an off-shoot of this movement there has been a substantial revival of the Better Business Bureau movement and the establishment of local NARBs.

Government Regulation

The first involvement by the government in the control of advertising came in 1872 with the passage of post office laws designed to curb the use of the mails to defraud. There is no exact count of Federal Government agencies that participate in regulating advertising but the list keeps growing. Happily, occasionally one drops out of the regulatory picture, like the Federal Energy Administration which during the OPEC oil crisis in the 1970s, took it upon itself to forbid the oil companies use of hard-sell tactics for their products. Other examples of government regulation are the required statement "use only as directed" in many television commercials for proprietary drug products, and the complete ban on cigarette advertising on television which is now threatening to spread to all media.

Consumerism and Special Interest Groups

Self-designated consumer advocates are everywhere today and every major government agency has at least one on its staff. Add to these a large group of ivory-tower dwellers who seem to feel that every stream should flow with nothing less than distilled water and that the air we breathe should contain absolutely no particulates. Finally, add a liberal pinch of special interest people who feel it is demeaning to show a woman as a housewife or to show a minority group member working at a job at the lower end of the scale. Take all these people together and you have a small but very vocal minority who yell loudly enough so some political types are tempted to put unrealistic restrictions on advertising in order to "protect" consumers from perils of which they're not even aware, much less worried about.

To show what can happen, here is the problem encountered by an Ohio agency seeking to produce a TV commercial for a nine-inch rubber ball. The description is in the words of the agency's Creative Director.

> It was decided to use tried and true techniques—like emulating "Sesame Street," with lots of color, animation, and talking letters; use as voice-over a male talent who'd had a successful kids' TV show for years; use to represent the kids "The Singing Angels," a group of nationally known, well adjusted, all-American youngsters. The commercial was written, the audio track cut, and the animation done. The material was sent to a well-known Chicago production house and all hell broke loose.

> The production house had sent the commercial out for network clearance and called to advise us to scrap everything and start over. Apparently a group of energetic crusading Boston mothers, self designated ACT (Action for Children's Television), had gotten the ear of a federal regulatory body and NAB (National Association of Broadcasters) and the commercial was not approved.

> The first meeting with NAB showed just a few things wrong with the spot. "Sesame Street" and talking letters were forbidden; animation is not true life and hence *verboten*; no excitement, either visual or audio, was allowed; the time-tested TV personality used off-camera "sounded like a drill instructor hoarse from shouting at the children" and did not represent a true play situation. It did not meet the criterion that commercials aimed at kids must show real-life scenes and activities as they would appear to the eyes of other kids.

Like it or not, until the pendulum swings back to a more realistic balance between reality and wild-eyed daydreaming over unattainable goals, you, as an agency person, are going to have to pay attention to these points of view and thus limit your freedom as how best to serve your clients.

In summary, there are restrictions on your freedom in advising your clients. Some of them are specific and must be complied with; others are subject to interpretation. In the long run, however, the best way to avoid running afoul of most restrictions is to produce good, honest, believable advertising that is in good taste. In the hard glare of publicity in which our industry operates, anything less is quickly evident and in the long run, self-defeating.

II Agency Financial Operations

5

Figures You Can Steer by

Basic Operating Formula

No one can possibly run a business as highly personal and creative as an advertising agency by feeding standard percentages into a computer and letting it tell you how to spend your money. On the other hand, you can't be sure of running a successful operation if you completely ignore the accumulated experience of others and rely on luck and a fast infield to produce a profit at the end of the year.

Some target figures are a useful thing to have, as long as you recognize them merely as guidelines and not gospel, because spending less than you make, and thus showing a profit, is still the best definition of sound financial management. This is achieved either by holding down costs or by increasing revenue.

First, you must know how much you can expect to retain from each dollar you bill your clients to meet expenses and earn a profit. The table on page 13 gives the figures for a large number of agencies over a period of years. Look into this more closely because of two trends that exist. The first of these is that as agencies grow in size, the percentage of their billing converted into agency gross income declines. On the other hand, this percentage tends to rise as the years pass. Here are the figures:

Agency Size Group	Gross Income as a Percentage of Billing	
	1972	1985
1 Smallest	21.73%	24.44%
2	22.82	21.43
3	20.52	25.86
4	17.74	19.34
5	15.47	18.22
6 Largest	17.82	18.05
All Groups	20.72%	22.60%

Throughout this book, the basis on which almost all comparisons are made is the agency's gross income, so it is vital to know what to expect in this area.

A second basic figure you must know in planning and controlling your operations is the number of employees needed to handle each $100,000 of agency gross income. As you would expect, this figure becomes smaller as time passes and also as an agency grows. Here are the figures you can expect:

Agency Size Group	Employees per $100,000 of Gross Income	
	1972	1985
1 Smallest	5.37	3.32
2	3.84	2.19
3	3.72	1.80
4	3.27	1.63
5	3.14	1.49
6 Largest	3.42	1.40
All Group	4.07	1.68

Financial data for the last three years show that agencies on the average spent 67.44 percent of their income on payroll and related expenses and 27.16 percent on all other expenses, leaving a profit before taxes of 5.40 percent. Converting these figures to percentages of total expense (which, after all, is what you can control) the 67.44 percent of agency income spent for payroll and related expenses becomes 71.29 percent of total expense and the 27.16 percent spent on all other expenses becomes 28.17 percent of the total.

Experience with many agencies over a period of many years shows that a typical breakdown of an agency's total expenses would look like this:

Typical Breakdown of Agency Costs		
Payroll & Related Expense:		
Direct Payroll:		
Client Contact	20.88%	
Creative	17.60	
Implemental	12.28	
Total Direct Payroll		50.76%
Indirect Payroll		
General & Administrative	9.02	
Executive Overhead	11.51	
Total Indirect Payroll		20.53%
Total Payroll & Related Expense:		71.29%
Nonpayroll Expense:		
Client Service Expense	4.81	
Space & Facilities Expense	15.93	
Corporate Expense	6.14	
Professional Fees	1.83	
Total Nonpayroll Expense		28.71%
Total Agency Expense		100.00%

Agency profit goals can vary widely, and for a great many perfectly good reasons, but sound agency budgeting requires first setting the amount of profit you want to shoot for and then controlling your expenses so you come up with that profit. This table is designed to help you do that:

Target Agency Expenses for Various Levels of Profit				
Target Profit Level	5.00%	10.00%	15.00%	20.00%
Payroll & Related Expense	67.73%	64.16%	60.60%	57.03%
Nonpayroll Expense	27.27	25.84	24.40	22.97
Total Agency Expense	95.00%	90.00%	85.00%	80.00%
Profit Before Taxes	5.00%	10.00%	15.00%	20.00%

All these terms will be defined and described in detail later, but here it will suffice to point out that these are functional targets and the same man may spend part of his time in several different categories and have part of his salary charged accordingly. The more an owner pays himself for writing copy, the less he can pay a copy man. What salaries you can pay to executives depends entirely upon what they do and how many hours they spend on each of their activities.

Now, for an example of how this formula works for controlling agency operations and profit, let's assume you want to earn a profit of 10 percent of income. This means that you must set aside this 10 percent first and spend only the remaining 90 percent. You'd expect this to be broken down to 64.16 percent for salaries and 25.84 percent for all other expenses but, obviously, you can shift expenses at will between categories as long as you don't run over the 90 percent total.

A well-conceived and carefully run cost system is, of course, an essential when you run an agency in this manner. The cost system must show accurately the cost of each function performed for each client if it is to be the principal tool for the control of operations and profit.

Significant Ratios

Compiled here for ready reference is a list of the financial figures that are most significant and useful in controlling an agency's operations. Each is shown in the range in which you'd expect it to fall. Since every agency operates in a different way, these figures can only be considered as guidelines.

Guidelines for Expenses
Each of these expense guidelines is expressed as a percentage of total agency gross income.

	High	Low	Refer to
Payroll & Related Expense:			
Direct Payroll			Chapter 8
Client Contact	19.84%	16.71%	
Creative	16.72	14.08	
Implemental	11.66	9.82	
Total Direct Payroll	48.22%	40.61%	
Indirect Payroll:			Chapter 8
General & Administrative	8.57	7.21	
Executive Overhead	10.94	9.21	
	19.51%	16.42%	
Total Payroll & Related Expense	67.73%	57.03%	
Nonpayroll Expense:			Chapter 8
Client Service Expense	4.57%	3.85%	
Space & Facilities Expense	15.13	12.75	
Corporate Expense	5.83	4.91	
Professional Fees	1.74	1.46	
	27.27%	22.97%	
Total Expense	95.00%	80.00%	

Guidelines for Working Capital

The basic comparison for working capital is with total annual payroll. Other derived relationships are to gross income and billing.

	High	Low	Refer to
Working Capital as % of Payroll	27.5%	22.5%	Chapter 11
Working Capital as % of Income	16.5	13.5	
Working Capital as % of Billing	3.5	2.5	

Guidelines for Net Worth

The basic comparison for net worth is with gross income. From this is derived a relationship to billing.

	High	Low	Refer to
Net Worth as % of Gross Income	35.0	25.0	Chapter 11
Net Worth as % of Billing	7.0	5.0	

6

Billing, Income, and Profit

What Our Terms Mean

Are you confused by numbers that represent "billing" or "capitalized billing" or "gross income"? Does profit, when expressed both before and after taxes and as a "percentage of billing" or a "percentage of gross income," also present problems?

Billing

First, there is no real mystery about the simple term "billing" (or "sales," as it is sometimes called). This is simply the total of all the bills the agency sends to the client—bills for media at gross rates (that is, including commission), bills for advertising services and materials purchased from outside sources (including, of course, a markup or agency service charge), bills for layout, copy, and other work done by your own staff, and, finally bills for any retainers or other fees.

Well, you ask, if this is such a simple concept why doesn't everybody use it? There are two reasons. First, most of the dollars listed as billing pass right through the agency with hardly a pause. On media bills 85 percent is paid immediately to the media and on production bills generally between 75 percent and 80 percent is immediately paid. None of this money can be used for the agency's own operations and hence does not truly reflect the size of the agency as a business enterprise.

Second, some kinds of billing dollars are worth more than others as far as the agency's operations are concerned. Out of every media dollar the agency retains fifteen cents to help meet its expenses; out of the production dollar it keeps about twenty or twenty-five cents; out of the fee dollar it keeps one hundred cents. So, before you can use a billing figure to compare one agency with another, you have to know what makes up the billing of each of them.

Capitalized Billing

To get around this problem somebody devised the concept of capitalized billing. This means, simply, that you take any billing for fees and multiply it by some factor to get a capitalized billing figure large enough so that the fee actually received equals the gross income normally received from the capitalized billing. The joker here is that this practice is really nothing but a mathematical exercise by which you can make the capitalized billing almost anything you want depending on the multiplier you use. The most common one is 6.667 which makes the fee equal to a gross income of 15 percent on the capitalized billing.

The table on page 36 shows that the gross income in 1985 for all agencies was 22.60 percent of billing. The proper multiplier to capitalize this rate of gross income is 4.425 not 6.667 so the use of the traditional multiplier substantially overstates billing.

To illustrate the absurdity of this whole concept of billing as the measure of the size or importance of an agency, let's consider an agency that operates strictly on a fee basis (which seems to be a growing trend) and sends its clients fee bills totaling $1 million. If billing as defined above is used as the criterion, this is a $1 million agency, but if it adopts a capitalized billing basis, it suddenly becomes a $4.425 million agency or a $6.667 million one depending on the multiplier the principals decide to use . Actually, this is a $1 million business because that's all it has out of which to pay expenses and taxes, and return a profit to the owners.

So, I strongly recommend the abandonment of billing (which is confusing) or capitalized billing (which is fictitious) as measures of agency size and use, instead, the agency's gross income. This same approach has been taken by the American Association of Advertising Agencies which for the years 1970 and earlier classified its members on the basis of billing; in 1971 showed both billing and gross income; and in 1972 started classifying on the basis of gross income alone.

Gross Income

As pointed out above, gross income is the total amount of money the agency has to meet its own operating expenses including compensation and profit for its owners. The customary definition is that gross income is the total of:

- Commissions from media (and infrequently from other suppliers) retained by the agency, *plus*

- Markups or other percentage charges added on to suppliers' bills by the agency, *plus*

- Amounts billed for the time spent by agency personnel directly on behalf of the client, *plus*

- Fees billed by the agency.

Another way to arrive at the same figure is to take the total amount billed to the client for media, production (including any amounts for inside time), and fees and then subtract from that the amounts paid to media and *outside* suppliers for furnishing the materials and services for which you are billing your client.

Whichever of the two ways you prefer to determine your agency's gross income the result will be exactly the same.

Gross income as defined above is the same for every agency, so you have a valid basis of comparison. Also, it's the best method of specifying the actual size of an agency as a going business. For these reasons, throughout this book all figures concerned with financial operations will be expressed as percentages of gross income.

Profit

When we start to define profit we run up against the idiosyncracies of the Federal tax laws plus the fact that the average agency is a highly personal business, usually owned and operated by very few individuals. This makes it possible for these principals to arrange payments to themselves in such a way as to minimize the tax bite—highly commendable, but a situation that tends to distort profit figures as normally defined.

An extreme example of this situation is the opportunity offered to corporations that qualify to elect to be taxed basically as partnerships. Under this method (Subchapter S) the owners pay taxes on their relative share of the corporation's profits and the corporation ends up with no profit whatsoever since the relative share of each principal is paid to him as a bonus. If the individual owner's tax rate is lower than the corporate rate, it obviously saves taxes, but plays hob with operating comparisons between agencies.

Operating Statement

A profit figure can be drawn off at any one of three places in a normal operating statement. The following example will illustrate these places and make it easier to understand the meaning and use of each of them.

Let's look now at the meaning and use of these different profit figures.

XYZ Agency
Operating Statement

Total Billed to Clients	$5,000,000
Less: Paid to Media and Suppliers	4,000,000
Gross Income	$1,000,000
Expenses:	
Payroll—Principal Owners*	$ 80,000
Payroll—Staff	447,200
Non-Payroll Expenses	272,800
	$ 800,000
Gross Profit	$ 200,000
Less:	
Bonus—Principal Owners	$ 25,000
Bonus—Staff	95,000
Profit Sharing—Principal Owners	5,000
Profit Sharing—Staff	$ 25,000
Profit Before Taxes	$ 50,000
Less: Income Taxes**	$ 7,500
Net Profit	$ 42,500

*Principal Owners are usually defined as persons owning 10% or more of the agency.

**Income tax figures are for purposes of illustration only and are calculated at the rates that will be in effect when the 1986 tax law is fully implemented.

Gross Profit

This is very easy to define. It is simply the amount of money the agency has left from its operations, out of which to pay taxes and such optional benefits as year-end bonuses and profit sharing. How much this figure means, however, when comparing one agency with another depends on the business philosophy of the principal owners. Some prefer to operate by paying themselves only nominal salaries during the year with a whopping bonus near the end of the year. So, this particular measure of agency profitability is not of too great value for smaller agencies where one or two owners may represent a quarter of the total employees. Its value as an effective comparison increases as agencies grow. After an agency reaches the approximate size of the XYZ Agency which would be, typically, two principal owners and 16 staff employees the figure begins to take on real meaning as a measure of distributable profits.

Profit Before Taxes

This is the profit left after making all discretionary bonus and profit sharing payments and from which only Federal income taxes need be deducted before arriving at the final profit available for payment of dividends and additions to surplus. Presumably at this point you've made all the discretionary payments necessary to keep your key people — and yourself — reasonably happy. Except in very unusual cases this figure represents the best measure of an agency's operations.

Note two things about this figure. First, only Federal income taxes remain to be paid from it. When I say this I'm assuming that any state and city taxes have been deducted as part of regular operating expenses. This is proper because there are as many different bases as there are different taxing authorities and some of them are so constructed that some tax is owed even if you lose money! Also, to act as a measure of your operations, profits must be stated before taxes. There are many things completely unconnected with operations that can affect the total tax due and hence the net profit — tax loss carry-overs and nonoperating income to name just two examples.

Net Profit

This, too, is easily defined as the amount left over for the owners to use as they wish after all expenses and taxes have been paid. This is the figure commonly used for the listed stocks of major companies, but I don't think it the best one for agencies. It's too much subject to control by the principals who are practicing commendable tax planning.

Proprietary Profit

This is a new term designed to permit the evaluation of an agency whose owners regularly engage in tax minimizing. By it I mean the total of:

Salaries of Principal Owners, *plus*
Bonuses to Principal Owners, *plus*
Net Profit

The use of this concept will make allowances for the owners who adjust their own salaries up or down according to their personal needs for current income and the need of the agency to accumulate surplus.

I'll close this section by summarizing the terms that will be used throughout this book:

Gross income is the principal measure of agency size and all operating figures will be expressed as percentages of gross income.

Profit before taxes is the normal figure used to represent the results of operations.

Proprietary profit will be used as a measure only when dealing with areas (such as agency valuation for merger or otherwise) where tax planning may be a factor.

How Much Profit?

Twenty percent of income is what an agency should make, but published figures average a lot less. Why? If 20 percent is unrealistic, what should an agency earn?

This is a good question, but not one that can be answered categorically. You'll recall that in the introductory chapter of this section I didn't use a single formula, but developed a table showing typical major expenses at different levels of profit. You pick the profit you want to achieve and then control your expenses so you do reach it at the end of the year.

"Well," you say, "that's fine, but how do I know what my target should be? How do I know if the target I pick is reasonable or if I'm dreaming?"

First consider what profit is meant to do. There are three principal goals. (My list is not in order of importance because priorities are always changing and depend on the agency's stage of growth.)

One goal certainly is to build up the strength of your agency. Accumulate the necessary working capital and the resources to withstand normal short-term business crises. Give the agency a basis for seeking credit, if necessary, and the wherewithal to take any available discounts.

A second major need for profit is to pay the owners of the agency for their contributions to its operations and also to reward them for the risks of ownership they're taking. Of course you undoubtedly pay yourself a salary, but if you're like most owners of small agencies I know, you'll set your current salary at a modest level and then take from profit enough to bring your total up to what it should be. But to do this you must have a profit!

The other principal use for profit is to give a little extra reward to the guys and gals who've worked for and with you all year. This can be a bonus or profit sharing but, again, the profit has to be there first!

Well, you may say, how about Uncle Sam? He's surely going to share in the profits. True enough, but no one in his right mind would earn a profit just so he could pay some taxes. Paying taxes is not one of the purposes of making a profit but, rather, an involuntary sharing of profit. This, of course, modifies all the numbers, but there are many things you can (and should) do to minimize taxes.

So, to set your profit goal for the year, start at the bottom and work up. Figure out how many dollars you must set aside to increase the strength of your agency. Some guidelines relating capital to agency size are discussed in chapter 11. Let's say you settle on $50,000. This is 5 percent of gross income for the typical agency I've been using as an example.

This is net profit (that is, after taxes), so to get the corresponding profit before taxes, which, you'll remember, is the basic measure I'm using, you do a little mathematics based on the tax rate (15 percent in this case) and come up with a profit before taxes of $58,800. This is 5.88 percent of your $1 million gross income. So here's your starting point.

Profit Before Taxes	$58,800	5.88%
Income Taxes	8,800	.88%
Net Profit	$50,000	5.00%

How about reasonableness? Is the old 20 percent rule of thumb an attainable reality or a pipe dream? Let's look at the record compiled by agencies whose operating statements I have studied over a period of years. This chart shows an average profit of 3.86 percent of gross income.

The profits of these agencies were distributed as follows:

Profit Before Taxes as % of Gross Income	% of Agencies
Over 20%	4.48%
15% –20%	6.19
10% –15%	12.78
5% –10%	26.29
0% –5%	37.87
Lost Money	12.39
	100.00%

So 20 percent is an attainable goal. It may not be an easy goal to reach, but nothing really worthwhile is easy.

How Is Profit Divided?

In the last section I mentioned briefly the three major uses to which profits are put and said that the priorities between them vary with the stage of an agency's development. Let's look into each of these a little more closely.

Capital

When an agency is just starting out, the most important use for an agency's profit is to build up its capital to make it a sound business operation. You need working capital equal to about three months' payroll (or about 14 percent to 17 percent of gross income) plus enough to finance your few fixed assets such as furniture and typewriters plus some more to represent a cushion against temporary slow periods. All of these would indicate a need for captial equal to about 25 percent to 30 percent of your gross income.

Once you reach this figure you probably won't want to add much more capital except as it's needed to finance further growth. Remember, an agency is a people business, not a brick and mortar one. It's much more important to invest in people than to build a big surplus once you've built up enough to let you take any discounts offered and have a modest cushion against a rainy day. But remember that until you reach this point, it's of utmost importance to strengthen the agency by retaining profits.

Staff Rewards

Since the whole success of an advertising agency depends on its people, you have to keep them happy and productive — and this usually comes right down to a question of money. There are two general philosophies in this area. One is to pay your people what you have to — in your market and in these times — and pay yourself, as owner, whatever is left over. The other way (which I prefer) is to pay your staff on a day-to-day basis just a little less than they could command in the open market and then share with them an extra reward at the end of the year. This is a matter of personal judgment, but it's been shown that a modest part of profits devoted to sweetening the kitty for your people each year can pay big dividends in increased loyalty and productivity.

Ownership Rewards

The owners of most small- to medium-sized agencies are hard working sincere people who expect to take only enough income out of the agency each year to meet their current needs and still have some left over to build up the value of their investment in the business.

So, in fact, the owners' take from the business is a combination of current salary and profits retained in the business. Fortunately the tax laws offer a fair degree of latitude as to how you do this to give yourself the maximum combined income and retained agency profits while minimizing corporate taxes.

The things to take into account are the corporate tax rate and your own effective tax rate after counting all proper deductions, exemptions, and so on. Remember, as Mr. Justice Holmes pointed out, the law requires no one to pay one penny more tax than is due. Tax evasion is not to be countenanced but tax avoidance by following the letter of the law is financial planning of the highest order.

7

How Agencies Are Paid

It is well established nowadays that advertising agencies have to gross more than the 15 percent on billings of the so-called commission system. What is not clear, however, is what services come under the remuneration provided by commissions and what extra ones have to be charged for in the form of fees or markups beyond this set percentage. Is there any well-established procedure accepted by agencies and clients alike, or is it still quite indefinite? Do agencies just charge what they can get? If so, isn't this a self-defeating practice?

As I pointed out in chapter 2, there are only two ways in which you, as an agency principal, can have any influence on profit. One is to increase agency income, or at least see to it that income is reasonable in view of the services you offer, and the other is to control expenses. There just isn't any other way to affect profit. This chapter will cover the first of these factors — agency income — and the next chapter will talk about expenses.

The opening question indicates all the ways in which an agency can get paid for its services, and thus, serves as a splendid introduction to the problem of agency compensation.

To answer the broadest part of the question first, before branching out into a discussion of the different major ways in which an agency is paid for what it does, it is absolutely right that an agency today must gross more than the so-called standard 15 percent. Throughout this book I've been using 20 percent as a standard and this seems to be borne out by industry figures. Don't forget, though, that if total agency income is to be 20 percent of billing, the income from some activities must be far more than 20 percent to keep the total up to that level.

Commissions

Let's look first at just one part of the question that started this chapter: "What services come under the remuneration provided by commissions?" The answer to this question must be that commissions from media make up part of the income of most agencies and help to pay part of the cost of every service the agency provides. Way back in the beginning it might have been possible to say exactly what services media commissions paid for, but in today's complex multi-service agency it's really a meaningless excercise to try to say what source of income is supposed to pay for what service in whole or in part. What is important is the total agency income, not where it comes from.

For many years now media commissions have been standardized at 15 percent, with two major and some very minor exceptions. The two major ones are outdoor and transit advertising, where the commissions run 16-2/3 percent, and local rate advertising where no commission is allowed. In the latter case the almost universal practice is to gross it up by billing at the net local rate plus 17.65 percent to give the agency its 15 percent on the amount the client ends up paying.

Thus, with very few exceptions, the agency can expect an income of 15 percent on all the media it buys and clients are accustomed to paying on this basis. It's almost unheard of for a client to object to any media bill assuming that the reproduction or other physical characteristics weren't fouled up, and that billing was at the scheduled rate. At the same time, you can't realistically expect an increase in the rate of media commissions because agencies are not doing anything for media that they haven't been doing for years. No increase seems warranted.

Even when an agency is compensated completely by fees, the mechanics are usually such that normal media commissions are paid to the agency and then credited against the fee. So, in a nutshell, the commission system seems here to stay as a base, as an income-producer for some of the agency's services; but it must be supplemented by fees or additional charges of one kind or another to cover the additional services needed in modern, highly competitive marketing, which only the advertising agency can perform so well and at so low a cost to the advertiser.

Markups

In spite of being used for many years there still seems to be some confusion about the 17.65 percent markup. What is a simple explanation? Also, to what kind of items do you usually add markups?

Both 15 percent taken off the gross media bill and 17.65 percent added on to a net bill produce exactly the same 15 percent income to the agency based on what the client pays. It's just the difference between discount and markup. Maybe a table will simplify the explanation.

	Commission Basis	Markup Basis
Billed to Client	$ 100	
Less: Commission	− 15	
Cost to Agency	$ 85	$ 85
Plus: Markup		+ 15
Billed to Client		$ 100

Thus, no matter how you figure it, the client pays $100 for something that costs the agency $85. When you start your calculation with cost you have to add $15 to reach the same bill to the client and this $15 represents 17.647 percent of the $85 cost to which it is added. It's just that simple!

I know one agency that uses this language in its client agreement:

> We charge an amount which, when added to the net cost of media allowing no commission or less than 15 percent commission, will yield us 15 percent of our total media bill to you.

What's Marked Up?

Now let's turn to the question of what items are marked up and which are normally billed net. Generally, advertising materials and services purchased from outside suppliers are marked up. This category includes all the necessary mechanical elements that go into the final ad — artwork, electros, and printing, for example, plus all the incidental steps taken along the way — photostats, retouching, and keylines, to name a few. The same is true of broadcast advertising except that here you may find a station selling both time and talent as a package, in which case the whole thing is usually subject to commission.

At the other end of the scale is a list of things that agencies never (well, hardly ever) mark up. These are all those out-of-pocket expenses incurred for specific clients that you simply try to recoup — such items as postage, long-distance telephone charges, and travel. The one major item to which you never add a markup is a charge for time spent by any of your own people. It just makes no sense to bill $25 for an hour of an artist's time and then add a 20 percent markup when it's so easy to increase his rate to $30 and forget the markup. When you control the price, it's silly to irritate the client by adding on a markup when you can simply increase the price.

Then, finally, there's a big middle ground where no universal custom exists. Here you find such things as billing for research studies and store checks which you'll have to play by ear. If it's a relatively small job you'll probably add a markup to the outside costs. If it's a big one you'll probably give your client a package price into which, of course, you'll build a markup for yourself.

How Much Markup?

"All this is fine," you say, "but what markup do I add to different items?"

There are two schools of thought on this. One school charges the same markup on all outside purchases and makes up the balance of needed income by adding fees of one sort or another. Agencies that follow this philosophy never mark up less than 17.65 percent and, in an increasing number of instances, use 20 percent, 25 percent, or even 33-1/3 percent.

The other school uses different markups for different kinds of jobs. Most of this group would use 17.65 percent on production to be used in media advertising, some would increase this to 20 percent for production used for low-cost trade paper advertising, and most of them would use 20 percent or 25 percent on collateral jobs.

Even when agencies use this method they'll probably have some supplemental fees for different kinds of work. I prefer this policy of using different markups for different kinds of work. It ties the agency compensation much more closely to the work the client requires and thus is more equitable and easier to justify than a single flat markup.

So, while I can't provide a specific markup percentage, or even a series of them, I can point out one general principle that may help you set your own charges. This is that the farther you get from media advertising, the larger the markup needed. Almost everyone marks up noncommissionable media by 17.65 percent to come up with the normal 15 percent commission on all media. In trade magazine advertising the media is usually inexpensive and can't carry as large a percentage of the agency's cost, so the markup on production of trade ads tends to be somewhat higher. At the extreme end of this range of services is a collateral job with no media commission to help foot the bill, so the markup is almost always higher and is usually supplemented by a fee to boot.

Internal Charges

Does charging by the hour mean instead of, or in addition to, the 15 percent arrangement? How should this practice be carried out?

There is no questioning the fact that, with increasing costs for running an agency, the squeeze is on the commission system. We must either operate on a straight retainer basis, charging fees for our services, crediting our allowances from media against such fees to the client, or we must supplement our revenue from commissions by additional charges.

Charges in addition to commissions are of various types. The simplest, and perhaps the most widespread, is charging for layouts done by your own internal staff, even on commissionable accounts. Most of the smaller agencies and many of the largest do this.

Most agencies feel that an integral part of their service to clients, for which they are compensated by media commissions, is the development of the creative concept. By this they mean the writing of any copy and the production of a layout that is sufficiently finished so the client can visualize and approve the concept. If the client isn't sophisticated enough to work with a rough layout, or if he wants something fancier for management, most agencies feel he or she should pay for it. So, if any comprehensive or semi-comprehensive layouts are needed, the agency feels justified in charging for them, even if they are made internally. Some agencies even charge for rough layouts, particularly when they're for industrial clients in low-cost trade magazines.

Many agencies also charge for writing copy — again especially in the case of industrial clients in which the copy may be long and technical.

There's a long list of assignments given to agencies for which there is no media commission whatsoever. At the head of the list are collateral jobs such as catalogs, brochures, and annual reports. If there's a big print run that the agency gets to handle, maybe the markup on that will be enough to cover costs and produce a profit, but chances are the client will handle the printing directly. So the agency must charge for the time all (and I mean *all*) of its people put in on the project.

Other activities the agency staff may be asked to undertake and that must be paid for under special arrangements would include complicated promotional jobs consisting not only of difficult and expensive-to-prepare technical trade advertising, but also elaborate point-of-purchase materials, publicity releases, and even general public relations counsel. For such jobs, the agency must receive a fee or find itself badly in the red at the year's end.

How to Pay for Internal Charges

I've said it before, but it's so basic it bears repeating — all any agency has to sell is the time and talent of its people. So, the agency's cost of one of these jobs handled internally has to be based on the time used by different people and their salary levels (as an indicator of their talent).

Hourly Rates

The simplest and most direct way to charge for internal time is by using hourly rates applied to the time each person spends on the job. Each employee's hourly rate is customarily based on a standard year of 1,600 hours (which allows for vacations, holidays, a few days home with the flu, and coffee breaks) and his basic hourly rate is his salary divided by 1,600. So, a $32,000-a-year man has a basic rate of $20.

There's more to it than this, however, because every one on the staff generates overhead; hence, each dollar of direct salary is charged with its proportionate share of overhead. I'll talk about overheard at some length in the next chapter, but at the moment let's say that each $1.00 of direct expense has to carry $1.174 of overhead—which is a pretty good average. The real hourly cost of our $32,000 man, then, is $20 plus $23.48 or $43.48. But, this is just your cost and you want to make a profit.

If you're shooting for the recommended 20 percent profit on gross, you'll have to mark your cost up by 25 percent (the same old 15 percent vs. 17.65 percent gambit) and this adds another $10.87 to the hourly cost. All of which gives you a billing rate of $54.35. At 2.718 times basic salary this is well within the range of 2.5 to 3.0 that many agencies use as a multiplier to convert salaries into billable rates. By all means adopt some such standard multiplier if you wish, but be sure to check it first by following the procedures discussed in chapter 10. Every agency is different in how it keeps its records and accounts for its time, so don't run the risk of shortchanging yourself by not checking first.

Standard Prices

Some agencies prefer to establish a standard price list for different kinds of layout, based on their past experience and a check with art studios in their market to see that the prices are competitive. Such a list can show as many prices as you want for different sizes, number of colors, and other art-related matters. Its great virtue is that it's simple and uniform. It eliminates possible embarrassment (or, worse yet, write-offs) when one layout takes twice as long (and hence costs twice as much) as another that looks almost identical. If you're careful about building the price list, you'll come out as well as, or better than, charging by the hour. This approach is particularly applicable to layout but can be applied to some kinds of copy (a standard catalog page, for example).

Creative Fee

Many agencies I know normally charge a creative fee in addition to the other forms of charging for internal services. This is usually meant to cover the services of the top creative people who will be involved in general supervision of the creativity on a project even though they devote almost no direct time to it. It's usually expressed as a flat dollar charge per job.

Job Fee

Some kinds of jobs, particularly large research projects, can best be paid for by means of an overall fee worked out in advance with the client. Such a fee should cover the cost of services supplied by outsiders, reimbursement for the time your own people will put in on the job, and, of course, a profit for the agency. When working out such a fee, be very careful to spell out who is to do what and provide for some kind of adjustment or escape hatch in case conditions change.

In summary, I feel, by and large, that charging hourly rates for the hours actually devoted to a specific job is the best way to be reimbursed for time spent internally on billable activities. It's a system that can be used under any circumstances and it's one that insures the agency of a profit on every hour that's billed. The other methods mentioned meet specific needs but, in the long run, are far less flexible.

Retainer Fees

Accountants, doctors, lawyers, and other professionals all charge their clients fees for professional services. Why don't advertising agencies do the same thing? The answer goes way back to the early days of agencies when they were really space brokers and in no sense professionals. As their business became more complicated and they were called upon to supply more and more specialized services, agencies increasingly took on professional aspects.

So, when agencies were forced to increase their income to meet rising costs, most of them turned to fees either as a supplement to income from commissions and markups or as a replacement for them. I think this is a growing trend and know of at least one multi-million dollar account that's handled on an overall fee basis.

In the previous section I wrote about fees charged for certain types of jobs and others, such as creative fees, used for specific projects. What I'm talking about here is an overall retainer fee. This kind of fee can be in addition to all commissions, markups, and charges for inside time that the agency retains, or it can be much larger, completely replacing all other sources of agency income. It doesn't really make any difference so long as the total income compensates the agency for what it does and gives it a profit.

How Are Retainer Fees Calculated?

The classic retainer fee is stated as so much per month or year or whatever period you wish. Its amount is usually set by mutual agreement between the client and the agency. But this is just the end product; you'd better have some hard facts and figures to back you up in negotiating the fee. Your cost system, covering your overall operations and those on behalf of the client, must include these figures:

- An estimate of the salary cost for the time needed by the right number of the people with the skills necessary to do what the client needs to have done.

- An accurate estimate of the overhead associated with the salary cost.

- A provision for take-home pay for the principals that bears some resemblance to what they could earn in the open market. (This is calculated as part of the overhead factor.)

- Enough year-end profit to let you meet your goals.

How About Adjustment?

It would be a major miracle if the fee agreed upon by you and your client produces even a reasonable facsimile of the expected profit, no matter how good your intentions and how accurate your record keeping. Plan from the beginning to review the fee periodically and make any adjustments necessary. It will be easier to do this if you and the client have agreed on exactly what the fee covers: services to be performed, the people who will be involved, and the number of hours they will spend on the project.

If you set down exactly what you will provide in time and services, you can provide for adjustments with a clause like this one in your agreement:

> The fee should provide the Agency with a profit before taxes of 15 percent of the amount billed to the client:
>
> a. If the profit exceeds 15 percent, half of the excess will be refunded.
>
> b. If the profit is less than 15 percent, the agency shall receive a supplementary fee equal to half of the deficiency.

Another adjustment clause says simply:

> The agency's monthly cost accounting report, based on individuals' daily time sheets, will be the basis for the fee computation.

Other Ways of Figuring Fees

Besides the mutually agreed upon fee, there are two other common ways of setting up an overall retainer fee. The first might be called *hourly rate fee*. This is exactly the same as the method previously described for billing for services performed by artists, writers, and the like. The only difference is that when billing is on a total hourly rate basis, the time of every one from the boss to the mail room boy is tallied and billed.

The other fee method is *cost plus*, under which all agency expenses including time and out-of-pocket are totaled, a profit factor is added, and the total is billed as a fee.

I don't really like either of these methods, basically because of the invitation to inefficiency and waste that's inherent in any cost plus system. But they do exist and, if properly controlled, can ensure a profit for the agency — if it doesn't go overboard and lose the whole account.

You Must Have Supporting Data

The minute an agency starts charging for anything more than commissions and strictly mathematical markups, that is, as soon as it starts to bill for inside time and any sort of fee, it should be prepared to justify its charges with facts and figures.

The first requirement, without which no amount of facts will prevail, is to have a satisfied client. He or she must be convinced that your knowledge of his business, your professional skills, and your diligence in applying them on his behalf are giving him the kind of counsel best suited to his business needs. With this favorable client attitude the battle's half won; without it, you'll soon lose the account anyway.

I've already mentioned the second requirement — a sound cost system. In addition to providing the basis for estimating and setting fees, it's an absolute necessity for justifying your charges. At some point even the happiest client, probably prodded by auditors or stockholders, is going to ask you to justify a fee. Some agencies I know beat the client to the punch and regularly go over with him their cost figures on his account. If you're sure of your figures (and don't do it if you're not!) this can build confidence and goodwill and may even get you an increased fee if your profit isn't all it should be.

The last, but probably most important, kind of support you need is a system of accurate time records showing who spent what time on which account. This brings us back to the fact that the time and talent of its people is the only thing any agency has to sell. If you don't know how your time is used, you're flying blind and can't charge clients what you're entitled to charge.

Of course, keeping accurate time sheets presents a problem. Agency personnel, usually enthusiastic and emotional, don't like numbers and hate to run in financial harness. Well, tell them that the one bunch of numbers they're sure to like — those on their paychecks, bonuses, and profit sharing — depends entirely upon the agency's knowing how much money it is making, and that it operates in the dark without their cooperation in turning in accurate time records. Don't expect them to keep accurate time sheets just because you tell them to do so. They won't. They will, however, if their personal interests are involved.

The ultimate in time recording systems is the installation of a time clock for each artist. When a newly hired art director was introduced to his own personal time clock, his predictable reaction was, "You've got to be kidding." This same man now tells me that the time clock is the greatest thing that ever came down the pike. He doesn't have to remember to write down what he does, he just takes the job card that comes to him with the job and puts it in the time clock when he starts work and again when he finishes. Somebody else figures out the time he spent and he doesn't even have to sign his name because his time clock has a distinctively colored ribbon that identifies him. Best of all he knows that every hour he works is recorded on the proper job number and that he will get credit for all the time he puts in when the jobs are billed. Finally, if somebody should question the time reported, there's the nice little card with numbers automatically printed on it. I talked to this guy and he's really enthusiastic!

Publish Your Terms

Most agencies, when making a presentation to a prospective client, suddenly become blushing violets when the time comes to let the client know what their charges are. Once it has been settled that the agency is desirable, from the client's viewpoint, and clearly capable of doing a good job, the question of financial arrangements should be tackled then and there; diffidence can only cause trouble later on. Actually a client can feel only increased respect for an agency that insists on clarification of the financial arrangement before it concentrates on the professional relationship.

Not only should a well-run agency be happy to talk about its charges, it should have a price list (often called standard billing terms) printed up for distribution to all clients. This is a measure of professionalism that saves a lot of headaches. A client will pay almost any bill if he's expecting it; it's the unexpected bill that causes trouble.

An outstanding example of a price list (called "Working Arrangement" by the Chicago agency that uses it) is broken down into six broad functional areas:

- General Advertising

- Sales Promotion

- Publicity and Public Relations
- Research and Market Analysis
- Special Assignments
- Postage, Telephone, and Telegraph charges.

Each of these broad areas is subdivided into the different media or materials involved and the service to be performed with regard to each. The charge for each is then clearly shown as no charge, net cost, standard hourly rates + cost of materials, or creative fee as the case may be. This list covers six full pages and is supplemented by a dated sheet showing current hourly rates for different functions. There should be no unexpected bills from this agency!

Summary

The whole question of agency income turns out to be not a series of rigid percentages or methods of charging, but a set of basic financial management principles:

- Determine the income you need to cover expenses and provide a reasonable profit.
- Choose any combination of income sources — commissions, markups, internal charges, or fees — that will work best in your market and for your particular list of clients; and remember each client can be handled on a tailor-made basis if you want.
- Have a record keeping system that will unmistakably prove the correctness of your charges.
- Tell your client ahead of time what your basis of charging is, review operations with him periodically, and show a willingness to make adjustments so the charges are fair to both you and the person who pays the bills.

Wise advertisers select agencies that offer outstanding abilities in advertising and marketing. They expect the agency's output to reflect these abilities in originality, initiative, and sound reasoning.

As in all things, in the long run you get what you pay for. Just as advertisers need to realize that cheap advertising services are invariably the most expensive in the long run, so agencies must recognize their own value and refuse to sell themselves for less money than can show a decent profit.

Clients that do not provide an agency with a reasonable profit must have their charges increased or be dropped. The only alternative, if the agency is not to lose money on these clients, is to cut down on services. This hurts both the advertiser and the agency in very short order. Only the best advertising succeeds in these increasingly competitive days.

In conclusion, set your profit first, charge enough to produce it, and above all, be ready to prove unmistakably that your charges are justified. Any client who is not willing to pay fair sums for services rendered should get another agency.

8

How Agencies Spend Their Money

An agency's basic philosophy should be to set aside profit first and spend on operating expenses only what's left. How should you classify these expenses and what are reasonable standards for each of them?

First, this basic philosophy represents the only way an agency can be sure of making a profit. This holds true even if a year comes along, as it will for most agencies, when good business judgment tells you that some things may be more important, that year, than a profit. Like keeping on a few key people even in the face of reduced client budgets so you can keep up your standards of service. The point is that you're on solid ground only if you make that decision with your eyes open. That way you're still in control.

The last chapter discussed the different sources of agency income; this one concerns operating expenses, the only other factor that has an effect on profits. This is probably the most important factor in planning for profit because you have much greater control over expenses than over income.

Total Expenses

Once you've determined the profit you want to make, you have also decided what your total expense will be because formula is:

$$Income - Profit = Expenses$$

There are two ways in which this total expense is broken down for purposes of control. They are, first, Payroll and Nonpayroll Expenses; and, second, Direct and Indirect Expenses. These two classification systems overlap, but they serve different purposes and each is vital to sound agency management. Basically, the Payroll/Nonpayroll breakdown is used for budgeting and controlling the agency's operations as a business. The Direct/Indirect breakdown is used for cost accounting to determine and control operations on behalf of specific clients. Each of these is discussed in the remaining sections of this chapter.

Payroll Expense

Agencies, after all, are only people and, as you'd expect, payroll is far and away the major item of expense. For the years 1983 to 1985, agency expense for payroll and related expenses averaged 71.29 percent of gross income.

So when you're setting up your budget, first decide how much profit you want, then figure out from the table in chapter 5 approximately how much you can spend for payroll based on your indicated income. Set that percentage as your goal and watch it like a hawk each month. All agency expenses are related to people and if you keep the people expense in line, chances are everything else will be in line too, including your profit.

A word of warning here. We never seem to learn, as engineers did long ago, to allow what is wisely called a margin of safety. Experienced in the cussedness of inanimate objects, engineers figure as closely as possible what stresses and strains will be encountered and then add a liberal percentage to take care of the unexpected.

Who ever heard of a bridge engineered to carry only the load it is expected to handle? If bridge builders figured that way, the mortality among bridges would be formidable, yet advertising builders figure only on what they expect to happen and if they modify their figures at all they do so in the direction of optimism. Instead, take 10 percent off expected income, putting extra profit into the bonus fund at the end of the year.

"Fine," you say, "we now have a total payroll figure, but how do we divide it among our people?" Here I can supply only guidelines because every agency is different and in all but the largest, many people wear several hats. Let's start by converting the 70.71 percent of total expenses represented by payroll into the percentages of total payroll for each function.

Typical Breakdown of Agency Payroll & Related Expenses		
Direct		
Contact	29.29%	
Creative	24.69	
Implemental	17.23	
Total Direct		71.21%
Indirect		
General & Administrative	12.65	
Executive Overhead	16.14	
Total Indirect		28.79
Total Payroll & Related Expenses		100.00%

A definition of each of these functional payroll categories follows:

Client contact. Includes the formulation of plans, and usually merchandising and public relations.

Creative. All art, copy, and radio/TV production.

Implemental. Includes all those activities necessary to get the advertising message into the medium, such as media, print production, research, and traffic.

General & Administrative. All those activities necessary to keep the office running, practiced by such people as accountants, billing clerks, messengers, receptionists, switchboard operators, and the like.

Executive Overhead. Includes the time the boss spends in directing the operations of the agency. This category also includes time spent on new business by all staff members. If you want to show this separately, fine, but it must be combined with other administrative payroll for purposes of analysis.

Secretarial. The one large group not included so far is the secretarial staff which is handled in one of two ways. Smaller agencies tend to list them as general administrative people while larger ones usually put them in the same category as their bosses. Philosophically I prefer the latter simply because I want to have the minimum dollars reported as general, but there comes a time when it just isn't worth the trouble to break down salaries of this kind. So, take your choice.

There are two ways you can list payroll figures to compare them with these guidelines. The man who does nothing but write copy is easy—he goes under Creative no matter which method you use. But the three-headed guy who contacts the client, writes some copy, and handles the media recommendations presents a problem. You can list him under what you think his primary function is and ignore the others for budget purposes or you can make an approximation of how he divides his time and divide his salary the same way—maybe 45 percent to contact, 30 percent to creative, and 25 percent to implemental.

If you use the method of putting a man's entire salary in a single category, you should adjust the basic guideline figures accordingly to reflect your method of operation.

When you use the proportional method, to some extent you're playing games, but I strongly recommend it for two reasons. First, the categories represent basic functions that every agency must perform and you should know what it costs to perform each of them. Second, this is the way in which industry figures are usually reported; hence, doing it this way will give you a valid basis of comparison.

If you use this recommended functional basis you can expect to pay for each function within these percentages of gross income:

Client Contact	16.7% – 19.8%
Creative	14.0% – 16.7%
Implemental	9.8% – 11.7%
General and Administrative	7.2% – 8.6%
Executive Overhead	9.2% – 11.0%

Of course, if you're at the high end of the range for one function you must be at the low end of others so you won't go over the total payroll percentage for the profit you're planning to make.

Whichever way you choose, be consistent and use the same system across the board.

In all of this, however, remember that every agency is different, so this sample distribution of payroll between different functions can be considered only as a guide. As long as you stay within the standard range for total payroll, you can shift payroll from one function to another at will, as best serves the needs of your clients. You can even make shifts between payroll and non-payroll expenses as long as you stay within the total expense figure you've set for yourself.

Nonpayroll Expense

This broad category generally represents just under 29 percent of an agency's total expenses and somewhere between 23 percent and 27.3 percent of its gross income. It is sometimes loosely referred to as overhead, but I think that's incorrect. There's a special section on overhead at the end of this chapter.

Just as people are expected to perform certain functions in the planning, creating, and placing of advertising, non-payroll expenses are incurred in the performance of certain functions vital to the operation of the agency as a business. There are four major functions of this sort plus the catchall "miscellaneous." By combining into these functional groupings the 20-odd expense categories that seem to be the accepted industry standard, we do away with the exercise in futility of riding herd on an expense item that may run one-tenth of one percent of income. For a typical agency with a gross income of $1 million, that's only $1,000 — so, even if that item increases by 50 percent it's gone up only $500.

Here are the major functional categories of non-payroll expense I like to use and a list of what goes into each. The categories are the same as are now used by the American Association of Advertising Agencies.

Client Service Expense

This category includes all expenses incurred for the benefit of specific clients. The major components are travel and entertainment and the cost of research and other items that cannot be billed to the client. The cost of these services should normally run from 3 percent to 6 percent of gross income.

Space & Facilities Expense

This expense provides for the physical surroundings in which you work. Rent is almost always the largest single item. You also include any maintenance or repair costs you incur, heat and light, a depreciation fund to replace worn out equipment, and insurance to shield you from losses. If you rent office machines, furniture or the like, you put those expenses here, too. If you own your own building — as many agencies do, particularly in smaller cities — you include mortgage interest, real estate taxes, and other costs of operating the building. Also included are the cost of such facilities and services as postage, telephone, data processing, and such items as stationery and office supplies, and the purchase of minor pieces of equipment. This category should normally run 13 percent to 17 percent of gross income.

Corporate Expense

This category represents the cost of general corporate activities such as the agency's own advertising, donations, provision for doubtful accounts interest paid, memberships, dues and subscriptions, and new business expenses. In total this category normally costs between 4 percent and 7 percent of gross income.

Professional Fees

This category covers fees paid to your C.P.A., your attorneys, and any other management service fees you may incur. It should run from 1 percent to 2 percent of income.

Summary

As with all the figures in this chapter, the ranges above are only guidelines that must be adjusted for each agency's operation. For example, if you move to suburbia, or even exurbia, to escape the high rent district, you can reduce your facilities expense, but as a result, you'll probably have to spend more on travel to see your clients, so that expense can be expected to go up. The important thing is to adjust as needed between categories to reflect your own operating style while keeping the total in line with your planned profit.

Thus, in a nutshell, the breakdown of total expenses into payroll and non-payroll categories lets you determine the total cost of each function performed by your people and also the cost of each physical function needed to provide tools and a place to work. At this point you're concerned with the function and its cost, not whether it is being performed for one or more specific clients or for the agency itself.

Direct and Indirect Expense

In addition to knowing what each agency function costs, it's important to know how much of the cost of each function is devoted directly to activities for specific clients and how much goes to keeping the agency running as a business enterprise. Without information of this sort you have no way of comparing the cost of handling a client's business with the income you get from it. Consequently, you can't tell which accounts are profitable (and by how much) and which are costing you money and require special attention.

This brings us to the second major way of classifying agency expenses-- direct expenses and indirect. Each of these categories will include some payroll expense and some nonpayroll expense. The distinction is that every item of expense incurred to serve a specific client is direct expense, while expenses connected solely with agency operations are classified as indirect.

For example, the president of an agency might spend 25 percent of his time contacting specific major accounts and another 10 percent in writing copy for those same clients. These, of course, are direct expenses. At the same time he may spend 30 percent of his time on new business activities and the remaining 35 percent in general administrative duties. Each of the two latter activities is considered part of executive overhead so each $1,000 of the president's salary would be distributed as follows:

Client Contact	$250	
Creative	100	
Direct Payroll Expense		$ 350
Executive Overhead (Indirect Payroll)		650
		$1,000

Almost every staff member will have both direct and indirect time and it's desirable to record the distinction whenever possible. About the only exceptions are accounting people, receptionists, and the like, almost all of whose time is indirect, though even these may have an appreciable amount of direct time.

On the other hand, an account executive who you'd think would have only direct time will have indirect time when he's pursuing new business or running some personal errands or just goofing off. You should try to segregate as much direct time as you can without carrying it to ridiculous extremes. It's particularly important if you have clients on a fee basis under which you bill at hourly rates for the time of all people involved with the account.

If you analyze the work of all staff employees the same way I did that of the principal owners, you might find this breakdown of each $1,000 of staff payroll:

Contact Staff:		
Client Contact		$ 750
New Business (Executive Overhead)		250
		$1,000
Creative Staff:		
Creative		$ 800
Administrative		100
New Business		100
		$1,000
Implemental Staff:		
Implemental		$ 850
Administrative		150
		$1,000
General Staff:		
Administrative		$ 700
Executive Overhead		300
		$1,000

Putting together the tables on pages 67 and 68, you would arrive at the breakdown of total payroll shown on page 69.

Most nonpayroll expenses are indirect, but some of large proportions can properly be classified as direct and charged against your operations for specific clients. The most obvious examples are long-distance telephone calls, travel and entertainment, and unbillables such as errors. It's important to isolate these costs of serving specific clients not only to figure total cost per client but also to bill for some expenses when they've been isolated and documented.

By definition, Client Service Expenses are always classified as direct expenses. Occasionally, however, some items of what is normally an indirect expense may be incurred for a special client project and should be moved into the direct category. If, for example, $500 of the telephone expense (normally included in Space & Facilities) was incurred for a specific client project, the total of nonpayroll expenses might look like this:

	Direct Client Expense	Agency Expense	Total
Client Service Expense	$45,700	—	$45,700
Space and Facilities Expense	500	$150,900	151,400
Corporate Expense	—	58,300	58,300
Professional Fees	—	17,400	17,400
	$46,200	$226,600	$272,800

Breakdown of Total Payroll

Function	Owners	Staff				Total
		Contact	Creative	Implemental	General	
Contact	$27,500	$128,175	—	—	—	$155,675
Creative	11,000	—	$124,960	—	—	135,960
Implemental	—	—	—	$99,110	—	99,110
Total Direct	$38,500	$128,175	$124,960	$99,110	—	$390,745
Administrative	$ —	$ —	$15,620	$17,490	$86,450	$119,560
Exec. O'hd	71,500	42,725	15,620	—	37,050	166,895
Total Indirect	$71,500	$42,725	$31,240	$17,490	$123,500	$286,455
Total Payroll	$110,000	$170,900	$156,200	$116,600	$123,500	$677,200

All of these statements of expenses can be combined into a single one that would look like this:

Direct Payroll Expenses			
Client Contact	$155,675		
Creative	135,960		
Implemental	99,110		
		$390,745	
Direct Client Expenses			
Client Service Expense	$ 45,700		
Facilities Expense	500		
		46,200	
Total Direct Expenses			$436,945
Indirect Payroll Expenses			
General & Administrative	$119,560		
Executive Overhead	166,895		
		$286,455	
Nonpayroll Expenses			
Space & Facilities	150,900		
Corporate	58,300		
Professional Fees	17,400		
		226,600	
Total Indirect Expense			513,055
Total Expense			$950,000

Overhead

This usually misunderstood and much maligned term is often interpreted as the place to put any expense that's difficult to classify. A little analysis of why we want to determine an overhead figure will simplify the problem.

Webster defines overhead as "those general expenses in a business which cannot be charged up as belonging exclusively to any particular part of the work." This implies, of course, that there are expenses that can be charged up exclusively to some particular part of the work and, furthermore, that such charges would be different for different parts of the work. So, before we can define overhead we must decide the part of the work to which it is related.

The total work of the agency is to serve its clients by counseling them and producing and placing their advertising. So, the different parts of the work would seem to be the services rendered to each separate client. On this basis overhead is the total of those agency expenses that cannot be charged to specific clients. In other words it is the same as the indirect expenses discussed in the preceding section. This includes, of course, both payroll and non-payroll items. So, if we credit the agency with gross income of $1 million, its complete operating statement would look like this:

Agency Income		$1,000,000
Direct Expense	$436,945	
Indirect Expense	513,055	
Total Expenses		950,000
Profit Before Taxes		$ 50,000

Whenever the word "overhead" is used in this book, I will be talking about total indirect expenses — those expenses not incurred for any specific client but on behalf of all clients as a group. How this figure is used in reports and how it is distributed will be discussed in the section on Cost Accounting in chapter 10.

9

Billing for Your Services

When Do You Bill?

An agency should not finance its clients' advertising; in other words, it should get paid before it is called on to pay media or other suppliers. How do you insure that your agency can do this?

I again want to emphasize the vital importance of getting your money before you're required to pay it out. An agency entrusted with spending $5 million of its clients' money would expect gross income of about $1 million, of which $677,200 would represent payroll. The generally accepted rule of thumb is that an agency's working capital should be about three months' payroll or, in this case, $169,300. This comes out to 3.38% of the agency's billing (or 4.23 percent of what it's committed to pay out to media and suppliers).

Put another way, the average agency has working capital equal to only about 1/24th of the amount of money it commits itself to pay out on behalf of its clients. If some of the agency's larger clients are seasonal advertisers it's quite conceivable that one month's total billing may come close to equaling the agency's entire working capital.

Any extension of credit (and this is exactly what the agency is doing when it signs on the dotted line for payments non-cancellable as of a given date, retaining this responsibility with no client money in hand until perhaps a month later) involves risk but extensions of this magnitude require extra caution. There are several precautions you should take.

First be sure that your letter of agreement, which states how you will serve the client, contains a sentence like this: "We will bill you for time and space so that we receive your payment before we are obligated for the amounts involved." In my experience, in nine cases out of ten this sentence—so vitally important to the agency's safety and survival—causes no argument whatever.

If the client should question it (and only if he does), it may be explained that the agency has the same policy toward all its clients, and that in handling small accounts, many of which cannot be protected by credit insurance, the agency must receive the funds involved before it can promise to pay them out. Otherwise, one single failure to pay on the part of an advertiser could well cause the loss of the agency's entire working capital.

Then, be sure that the timing of your billing is such that the client has enough time to process your bills in the normal manner and get the money to you on time. To do this, first decide when you want the money in hand, then set your billing date well before that.

Don't just adopt a standard lead time of 10 days or even 30 days, but do what a well-run Wisconsin agency head does. He adjusts the lead time to the particular paying cycle of each client. As he put it, "I had a cordial but frank discussion with our clients about billing space and time so payment is received prior to our obligation to media and they all understood. If a client had a 30 or 45 day pay schedule (after receipt of invoice) we advanced our billing that many days so we would receive their money in time to pay their bills."

Okay, but when should you expect to receive your money? Never—repeat, never—agree to wait to bill your client until you have been billed by the publisher or broadcaster and have received proof of performance in the form of tear sheets or affidavits of performance. By the time you get these and process them it will almost always be well beyond the due date on the publisher's or broadcaster's bill.

You should set the payment time for the date on which the advertising is irrevocably committed. In the case of print advertising this is the closing date, the date when the advertisement is on the press and there's no power on earth that can cancel or change that ad. So, a very strong case can be made for using closing date as the time when the agency and the client become liable to the publisher and when the agency should get its money from the client.

You may have some problems convincing long-time clients to go along with your new billing schedule, but you certainly should plan to bill all new clients on this proper businesslike basis.

If at the outset of negotiations with a prospective client, it becomes evident that he or she will not go along with this safe principle of agency management, watch your step. By demurring, the prospect is virtually saying, "No, we propose to use your credit, your money, to finance our advertising." This is not a good sign.

An agency just starting a business relationship will more easily establish the proper time of billing than one that has for years followed the risky road. It is admittedly difficult to go to established clients who have been paying regularly and ask them to pay earlier than has been their custom.

The best thing to do is to establish the safe and recommended method for all new clients, and endeavor tactfully to get old friends to go along with an evidently desirable practice, so far as the agency is concerned. So close are the relations between most agencies and their clients that often this shift is more easily achieved than you might believe.

It is not advisable to cut the timing too close. The due date on your invoice for time or space should be ten days before the closing date or the date of noncancellation. That gives enough leeway to explain that orders will have to be cancelled unless funds are received. I would hope, however, that the whole business has been so tactfully handled that this step will not be necessary.

Special Kinds of Media Billing

No agency in its right mind would think of billing on closing date for newspaper or spot broadcast ads, for that would mean a separate invoice for each ad. Furthermore, newspaper ads have a habit of shrinking and broadcast spots can be omitted or preempted or suffer power failures—so you don't really know what you have run until you get the proof of performance. In this kind of situation, is there any way to get your money? Yes, there is.

For these media adopt a one-line or commitment system of billing. Let's use TV spots as an example. At the end of the month you know what TV spots you have ordered, and the client knows, too, from his copies of the schedules. What neither of you knows at this moment is just how many spots ran, but there's no doubt that you and the client are obligated to pay for the spots that did run.

You look at your schedule and find that you've ordered, say, $3,250 worth of spots for November. So, on November 30 you send the client a bill (due December 10) that simply reads:

TV advertising Committed for November 19___ $3,250.
No stations, no dates, no times—just a single amount.

This bill carries your usual terms and, if he's well trained, the client pays it. During the following month you get all the station bills, check and audit them and prepare a completely detailed bill for the client. You send him this towards the end of the month and show a credit for the one-line bill he's already paid. Then you start all over with a new one-line bill at the end of this month.

What if there are always some omissions and the client objects to being billed for the full amount scheduled when he knows he'll get some of his money back? Easy. Just make the one-line bill equal to 90 percent of the commitment or whatever other percentage experience shows is about right for this client and his list of stations.

If the client says he doesn't want to pay in advance, point out to him that he's not paying in advance. He is irrevocably committed at the end of the month to pay for all the spots that ran during the month. The only thing is that no one knows exactly what did run and so you are billing him an estimated amount for the spots that already have run, that he has authorized, and is thus obligated to pay for.

Production Billing

Because production jobs can extend over several weeks, even months and because many different suppliers are involved, it's almost impossible to bill your client in time to get paid before you have to pay your suppliers. You just don't know which supplier is going to bill you when and in what amount. While you can't completely eliminate paying suppliers before you get paid, there are some things you can do to reduce the burden.

Progressive Billing
At the end of each month agencies using this system list each payment made to suppliers on each active job in the house. The client is then sent a bill for each active job covering payments made to suppliers for that job during the month just ended. This means that the agency must write a lot of bills and the client must accumulate several bills for many jobs, but it does substantially reduce the work-in-process inventory the agency must carry.

Inventory Billing
Some clients object to having to process all the bills issued under progressive billing and ending up with several bills for a single job. They prefer the single bill sent only as each job is completed. These client benefits can be retained and the agency still relieved of financing the work-in-process by using an inventory billing system.

Agencies that use this system list payments they make against each job number just as do those who use progressive billing. However, instead of sending out bills for these amounts, these agencies charge the amounts to an Inventory of Work-in-Process account with a separate listing for each job for each client. They then add up all the items listed for any one client at the end of the month and send out a bill that reads simply:

Inventory Accumulated for your Benefit at the
End of Month of _____ .... $7,460.

Any jobs that are completed during the next month are billed as usual and at the end of the month you send the client a credit for $7,460, and the new bill for whatever his inventory is then. So, you're really running a banking operation under which your client keeps on deposit with you enough money to finance his inventory.

Partial Billing

There's one other special kind of billing some agencies use on big collateral jobs that can go uncompleted for long weeks or months. Under this system you bill one-third of the estimated cost when the job is authorized, another third when the proofs are approved, and the final third when the job is finished.

Prompt Payment Problems

So, you've done everything you can to establish practices that insure your getting your money on time and still some clients drag their feet. Is there anything else you can do?

Friendly Persuasion

Most agencies I know rely heavily on the old theory that "the squeaky wheel gets the grease" and start calling the client as soon as a bill is due and not paid. Usually the account executive is given the responsibility for following through with clients. Make sure, though, that he or she realizes that the job is completed only when the money is in the bank and that, while the client must be pleased, the agency is of greater importance. That's where his paycheck comes from and where his first loyalty should be.

Other agencies have their financial people get in on the act at some point. Still others count on their principals. Whoever does this, have them keep at it. An agency's profit margin is too low to let things slide.

Cash Discounts

Many media have for years allowed a two percent cash discount for payment by the agency within 10 days. When agreeing to pass this on to clients, be firm in your policy that 10 days means 10 days. To avoid any misunderstanding, it's probably well to convert this into a specific discount date. Instead of saying "Cash discount of two percent if paid in 10 days" say right on your bills "Cash discount of two percent if paid by January 10th" or whatever date is applicable. When a client passes up a discount, get hold of his Treasurer and point out how much money he's losing by not taking the discount. Two percent for 10 days figures out to about 72 percent per year, and that ain't hay!

Credit Insurance

Credit Insurance is intended to protect you against non-payment of bills, but it can also help in cases of slow payment. A reminder to the client that your policy requires regular reports on past-due items can help speed things up.

Finance Charge

If a client wants you to act as a banker, he or she certainly should pay you for it. Like most department stores and major oil companies, many agencies are starting to charge 1 1/2 percent per month on accounts that are overdue. I urge you not to finance the client, but it hurts a little less if you get paid for it!

State Your Terms

I've said it before, but it's worth repeating. The bill that gives you most trouble is the unexpected bill. So don't keep your clients in the dark! When you're in the process of making your final pitch to a prospective client come right out in the open and say, "We charge for this and this; the basis on which our charges are calculated is thus and so; our terms of payment are these." No advertiser is going to object to this kind of approach; in fact, he or she will probably respect you all the more for taking a sound businesslike approach to questions about money. Go one step further and prepare a rate card that spells out all your charges and distribute it freely to clients and prospective clients.

10

Financial Reporting

Often an ad agency will find it practically impossible to get any idea of how it is doing financially, because the bookkeeper is so busy sending out bills and watching collections that he or she doesn't have time to draw up statements. The agency is audited once a year by an outside accountant and only then does it get any really accurate idea of where it is heading. Is this a normal state of affairs in our business and if so, should it remain this way?

The answer to this question must be, "Absolutely no!" An agency cannot know where it is going if its financial status is unclear. To chart a financial course properly you, as agency principal, must know at all times and as accurately as possible, just where the agency stands at any given moment and also how it got there over the past few months. This chapter will talk about the kinds of reports you must get, and when you must have them, if you intend to chart a sound financial course.

Regular Monthly Reports

Monthly reports are vital. It is astonishing how much can happen to an agency in only a month's time. The operation for this short period may amount to as much as the agency has in the world. An agency can be solvent one day and wake up the following morning and find itself bankrupt. Every advertising agency should receive, no later than the tenth of every month, a financial report on its situation. This should be considered part of the bookkeeper's job, whether this person is an inside employee or part of an outside financial service.

It is not enough to tell your bookkeeper, "We want to know where we stand, every month." Provide a simple printed form worked out with the aid of the accountant who is responsible for the company's yearly audit. The spaces on this form indicate the information that must be forthcoming every month. Without this form, the information could vary from month to month with no cohesion or continuity. Therefore, insist on getting these reports on the tenth of each month and don't accept any excuses. Here are the reports you should get every month without fail.

Operating Statement

Another common name for this is Profit & Loss statement. It should show the figures for the current month and also for the period from the start of your fiscal year to the present. If you operate on the basis of agency budgets (which I recommend), a third column should show the budget for the year to give you a benchmark to measure your progress.

This statement is designed to answer three simple, but vital questions:

How much income did we receive?
How much did we spend?
How much did we make?

First, how much income did we receive last month? Don't confuse this with billings. This figure is the total of commissions, markups, and fees received. It should be at least 20 percent of dollar billings, and even this may turn out to be too low. This figure is not profit. It is gross income. It does not include cash discounts because these we extend to the client as earned, in dollar amounts not percentages. If you wish, you may show the total amount you've billed your clients so you can check the percentage that gross income represents of the billing.

Likewise, you may want to show separately the income received from commissions, from markups, and from fees. But however you break it down for your own information, the important thing is to show total gross income which is the benchmark against which everything is compared.

Second, how much did we spend on our various services and our agency operations out of this income? These expenditures should be broken down to show separately each of the five payroll categories and four nonpayroll categories of expense discussed in chapter 8. By preparing your report in this form you can determine the percentage of gross income each major expense represents and then use these figures to check performance against the targets.

Third, how much did we make? Compare this each month with the profit goal you have set for the agency.

Balance Sheet

This is the statement that shows your financial status at the end of each month. Basically, it shows what you own and what you owe. Look critically at each of these figures, all the while asking yourself such questions as, "Are we really going to collect all those receivables or are we daydreaming? Have we really allowed enough depreciation so our figure for furniture and fixtures represents a true present value?" Be realistic in your answers, for if you're kidding anybody, it can only be yourself.

Accounts Receivable
This extremely valuable statement should be drawn up separately for each client and it should be aged. That is, list the oldest first. Go down this list with a firm resolve that you'll start screaming immediately about any items that are overdue. Don't let them build up!

Cost Accounting

The financial reports I've been talking about show how the agency as a whole is doing and how well cost relates to income for major functions. This is fine as far as it goes, but you also need some way of knowing which clients are showing a profit, and how much, and which are causing you to suffer a loss. In short you need cost accounting.

A good cost system shows not only which accounts are causing a loss (the accounts on which you should take corrective action) but also how much correction is needed. In addition, there is bound to come a time when you'll have to justify the fairness of the fees you charge clients. And there's no way you can do that if you can't demonstrate what your costs are. There are even some fee plans that call for adjustments based on cost accounting.

Basic Form
A separate cost accounting statement should be made for each client and should contain this kind of information:

Client A	Period	Year-to-Date
Gross Income	$50,000	$190,000
Direct Salaries	19,500	68,500
Share of Overhead	22,890	80,420
Direct Client Expenses	250	500
Total Expenses	$42,640	$149,420
Profit Before Taxes	$ 7,360	$ 40,580

When you've made a statement like this for every client, the total of the profit or loss shown for each must add up to the bottom-line figure on your operating statement for the same period.

Period Covered
Many agencies prepare cost accounting statements every month, but I don't think that's necessary except in unusual circumstances. Normally, a quarterly report is sufficient, in which case your two columns would be for the current quarter and for the period since the start of your fiscal year.

Direct Salaries
The sample shows only a single salary figure, which you'll want to break down to show the salary cost of each function you perform — such as contact, creative, and the like. The more detail you show the better control you'll have over your operations. Also, if you ever need to discuss fees with a client — and you probably will — you'll be on much sounder ground if you can specify what you did for him and what each function cost you.

Functional Time Sheets
The only way to tell how much direct salary to charge against each client is to have everyone who works an appreciable amount of time on an account turn in time sheets recording that time so it can be priced out. What you need to know is who spent how much time performing what function for which client. To have meaningful figures all these elements must be present.

Since you're concerned with functions, the time sheets must allow for recording not only the client served, but also the function performed. This means that a person who wears two hats must either use two separate time sheets, one for each function, or use a time sheet with different columns for different functions.

A final point about time sheets: they must be timely. It's awfully hard on Friday to remember accurately what you did on Monday, so the best system is to require time sheets to be turned in each day. If that can't be done, at least require that the time be recorded every day even if a longer period is covered by a single time sheet.

Direct Client Expenses
These are all those out-of-pocket items you have to incur in properly serving clients — travel, long-distance telephone calls, and charge-offs, to name just a few. Many of these items can readily be identified as being concerned with one specific client. They should appear on his or her cost accounting

statement so it will reflect your true cost of serving that client. It's obviously unfair to charge all clients for an expense incurred for just one of them, which is what you do when you leave such expenses in overhead instead of charging them against the specific clients who benefit from them.

Overhead

I've already defined overhead as the total of an agency's indirect expenses. It's very simple to arrive at the total overhead when you're preparing your cost accounting statements. You add up for all clients the direct salaries you've figured for each of them plus the direct client expenses and subtract this total from the agency's total expense. What's left is overhead.

Now comes the question of how you allocate this overhead to your different clients. The three most widely used bases are 1. gross income, 2. direct time in hours, and 3. direct salary costs.

The rationale behind allocation on the basis of gross income received from each client is that the agency's purpose in incurring overhead expenses is to receive income; hence overhead should be charged as that income is received. The big, and I think fatal flaw in this is that overhead expenses of an agency may bear no relationship whatever to income. A simple example will show what I mean. An agency may find that it can't handle a client's business at a reasonable profit so it seeks and gets a supplemental fee. The workload hasn't changed at all, no additional overhead costs are incurred, but the income the agency receives from this client has increased. So the client is penalized by being charged with more overhead and all other clients are benefited by overhead reductions. It can't really be justified.

The second widely used method is to allocate overhead on the basis of the hours of direct time devoted to each client. This is an improvement over the income basis because hours spent are related to work that must be done. This is all right for small agencies where almost everyone on the staff works on almost every account; unfortunately, it ignores the fact that some hours are worth more than others, whether in cost to the agency or value of services performed for the client.

The third method based on direct salary costs recognizes the different cost of hours put in by different people. Certainly an hour of the boss' time is worth more than an hour of the office boy's. It's also true that the boss generates more overhead. He has a big office, he may have two telephones, and he needs and uses more stenographic and clerical help. So there is a reasonable relationship between direct salary costs and the overhead needed to support them. What's more, the figures are readily available, which makes it simple to allocate the overhead. I advocate this method in all but very exceptional cases.

So, in practice, you would determine the total overhead and its allocation by this process:

Total Agency Expenses		$100,000
Direct Salary Expenses:		
Client A	$19,220	
Client B	15,190	
Client C	11,400	
	$45,810	
Direct Client Expenses	2,000	
Total Direct Expenses		$47,810
Overhead		$56,130

The $56,130 in overhead would then have to be allocated to the $45,810 of direct salary expenses and we would find Client A charged with $23,550, Client B with $18,612, and Client C with $13,968.

Estimating

Regular operating and cost accounting reports tell you quite accurately where you are, but they are of much greater value if they can be compared with a budget showing where you expect to be and, thus, how near you are to reaching your goal. This calls for a good estimating system.

Start by having each account executive estimate what income you'll get from each of the clients he handles. Have him estimate this by quarters. At the end of each quarter you'll know what income you actually received. Go over this record with the account executive, see where he has been unduly optimistic or pessimistic, and have him revise his estimate for the balance of the year. His accuracy should improve as he gets nearer to the end of the year.

Knowing not only what income to expect, but when to expect it will be a big help in evaluating the regular reports. If you're expecting only one-third of your income in the first half year, you won't be unduly depressed if your profit looks a little sickly after the first six months. It works the other way, too. If your estimates show two-thirds of your income in the first half year, a realization of this will cool your exuberance over a hefty profit and keep your enthusiasm from letting you approve all sorts of expenditures.

The ultimate test of a sound estimating system comes in setting a fee for handling a client's total account. If you and the client agree on what's to be done—so many ads of this or that kind, for example—and if you know from your experience and your cost system what it will cost you to produce this work, you can set an overall fee that will be fair to both you and your client.

Furthermore, with a realistic income and expense goal as a target you can tell at any time where you are. If things are getting a little out of kilter, your cost system should let you demonstrate this to the client, so you both can agree on a correction before things get completely out of hand.

Even if you aren't on a complete fee system with a client, but charge a fee only for some unusual jobs, a good cost system, and the accurate estimating of costs that it allows, is worth its weight in gold.

There are no areas in agency work in which a sound cost system is so essential as it is on jobs for which the agency plans to charge a fee. Not only will such cost accounting set up a remuneration fair to both client and agency, it prevents arguments and postmortems that could destroy the entire relationship. While one can safely advise agencies, particularly smaller ones, to work towards fee accounts for sufficient gross income, one must also add the hope that such work will not even be contemplated until the agency knows its costs and can prove them.

Schedule of Billable Hourly Rates

To let you bill a job on the basis of the hours put in on it, or to determine how large a fee should be to cover the work your people have put in, you must develop a schedule of hourly rates to be used for billing purposes. To give you the necessary income your billable hourly rates must cover:

Basic Salary Cost
Applicable Overhead
Profit

In the examples I've used in the cost accounting section of this chapter the agency's total overhead was $56,130 compared with $47,810 of direct expenses. So overhead is 1.174 times direct expenses. Also, for the purpose of setting billable rates, you should aim for a profit of 20 percent (which means a markup of 25 percent on cost).

If you apply these factors to an employee whose basic salary is $32,000 a year, or $20 an hour on the standard 1,600-hour basis, you calculate his or her billable rate as follows:

Basic Salary Rate	$20.00
Applicable Overhead	23.48
Total Cost	$43.48
Profit	10.87
Billable Rate	$54.35

You would bill this man's time at $54.50 per hour. Since the factors to cover overhead and profit are the same for all employees, you could calculate all your billable rates by using a multiplier of 2.725 to convert basic salary rates to billable rates.

You can use a separate rate for each individual based on his or her own salary or you can set single rates for groups of people. For example, you might bill all account executives at $81.75 an hour, all artists at $54.50, and all writers at $68.25. This grouping method is the one I prefer because it disguises individual salaries.

Once you've established your rates, I recommend that you take the final step of converting them to a schedule or rate card. This should be made available to all clients and should be dated so it can be revised from time to time as conditions change.

III Agency Finances and Ownership

= 11 =

What Is an Agency Worth?

Apparently, one of the most difficult questions to answer about our business is what an advertising agency is worth. The question keeps popping up in different circumstances. For example, if you're interested in buying an agency that's already operating, how much should you pay for it? If you bring two people into part ownership of your agency, should you give or sell them some stock? If so, how much? If you are looking towards a merger, how can you tell what your agency is worth, and what the other one is worth? A question closely related to all of these is, "What is a reasonable estimate of the minimum capital needed by an agency that bills about $5 million per year?"

How Much Capital Do You Need?

Let's start by answering the last question to set the ground rules for all the others. Any agency in today's economy must have gross income equal to at least 20 percent of billing. The days when agencies could operate on a straight 15 percent commission are long gone, if in fact they ever really existed. So, as a start, assume the agency will have gross income of $1 million.

The typical agency would spend 57.0 percent to 67.7 percent of this on payroll, both direct and indirect. Let's average this out at 63.4 percent of $634,000. It's also an old rule of thumb that it takes about three months from the time an idea is conceived, through production, billing, and all the other steps, until the agency gets the resulting income. So, you must be prepared to finance your payroll for this three-month period. This will require capital of $158,500. Also, there is furniture and equipment plus some work in process that can't be billed right now; so, this minimum capital should be increased to, say $200,000. There's one more complicating factor. If all your clients pay their bills on time (which means before you have to pay the media or other suppliers) all is well and good, but unfortunately clients are human and sometimes delay payment. So, to be on the safe side, tack on another $50,000 in capital so that your normal capital, if you want to sleep nights, is $250,000 or 25 percent of your gross income.

Times Earnings Basis of Valuation

So, the minimum value of our $5 million agency is $250,000 because that's what it has (or should have) in the bank. But anyone investing in an agency would want more than that—he or she would want future earning power to provide a return on the investment.

Normally you'd be willing to pay X times the agency's average profits, just as listed stocks are frequently quoted on a price/earnings ratio. A common rule of thumb has been that an agency's profit capability is worth from 5 to 10 times average after-tax profits. It is interesting to note that for the years 1976 to 1985 five publicly owned agencies reported in *Value Line* showed an average price/earnings ratio of 9.18. In the case of our hypothetical $5 million agency (or more properly $1 million business—see page 44) the gross profit before bonuses and profit sharing was $200,000 or 20 percent of gross income. After these two major distributions the profit before taxes was $50,000 or 5 percent of gross income. Taxes under the fully implemented 1986 tax law would be $7,500 leaving a net profit of $42,500. On the old 5 to 10 times profit formula, the agency would be worth between $212,500 and $425,000.

Before adopting this approach, however, think a little about the nature of an advertising agency. It is a highly people-intensive business where physical assets—bricks and mortar—have very little to do with its success. As Fairfax Cone once aptly remarked, it's the only business whose assets go down in the elevator every evening. This being the case, what makes the agency business succeed is what motivates its people and this may bear very little relation to the bottom line.

For instance, I know several agencies that, because the total tax bite on the owners would be less, choose to operate under Subchapter S. In this case all earnings are paid to the owners as dividends or bonuses and they pay the taxes personally with the result that the agency corporation has no tax and no profit whatsoever. At the other extreme is an agency whose principal owner could not buy life insurance and whose principal aim was, consequently, to increase the value of his agency's stock as rapidly as possible.

Given these two admittedly extreme examples one can conclude only that an agency's net profit after taxes is an extremely weak reed on which to base a valuation. It is too subject to manipulation in the best sense of the word.

One way to adjust for this situation and still retain the times earnings valuation would be to adjust the agency's profit and loss figures to what they would be if it operated in a normal manner. This, it seems to me, is nothing but an exercise that can only raise questions as to what is normal and what adjustments should be made to reach the normal figure.

Gross Income Basis of Valuation

It seems much more logical to base a valuation on known facts, that is, the size of the business or its gross income and its net assets and leave it up to the purchaser to retain as much or as little profit as his preferred methods of operation allows. This can, and probably will, bear no relationship to what his predecessor did. One well-known and tested formula relating future earning power to gross income has a maximum of 50 percent of a year's gross income.

If we assume a 16 percent factor, the earning power value of our hypothetical agency would be $160,000. If you add to this the $250,000 the agency should have as capital, you arrive at a total value of $410,000, which is well within the $212,500 to $425,000 range that results from using the 5 to 10 times profit basis.

So, no matter which approach is used, you come out just about the same. In either case, the particular point in the 5 to 10 times earnings range or the 0 percent to 50 percent of gross income range picked is based on a judgmental decision about the particular agency being considered.

Because the valuation based on times earnings requires an adjustment of those earnings to what they would have been, given normal operations (whatever that means), the valuation based on gross income does not. Thus, it seems the latter is the sounder basis to use.

Pay As You Go

There's one more important consideration, however, that stems from the very nature of the agency business. This is the complete dependence of the agency's existence on the length of time clients are likely to stay with the shop. Tenure depends not only on agency efficiency or even creativity but may be affected by developments in the client's organization or industry that are entirely beyond the agency's control. The personality of the agency owner and the account man is often vital to retaining business. The body chemistry between new agency management and long-term clients may be such that clients become disenchanted and leave — and the new owner who thought he or she was buying a vital going business may find he or she paid good money for an agency rapidly going downhill.

So any payment for future earning power based on past performance may really be buying a pig in a poke. How much more sensible for the purchaser (and beneficial tax-wise for the seller, also, if properly handled) to pay for future earning power only as it manifests itself over the years. A neat trick you say; how do you do that? Well, it's really very simple.

Let's extend our example one step further and assume that buyer and seller have both agreed that the price should be book value (or net assets or net worth) plus a premium for earning power of 16 percent of an average year's income.

Let's further assume that the payments for earning power will be stretched out over four years at the rate of 7 percent of the first year's gross income, plus 5 percent of the second year's, plus 3 percent of the third year's, plus 1 percent of the fourth year's. So, when the deal is concluded the buyer pays an amount equal to the agency's net assets, doing nothing more at this time than trading dollars. At the end of the first year he would make an additional payment equal to 7 percent of the gross income actually generated, and so on for each of the three remaining years.

For an illustration of just how this works let's go back to our hypothetical agency with billing of $5 million, gross income of $1 million, and net worth of $250,000. Let's also assume the 16 percent factor for future earning power. If the transaction were made at one time and based on past performance, the price would be 16 percent of $1 million or $160,000 plus $250,000 for net assets, or a total of $410,000. This could be a bargain or a calamity depending on whether the future earning power was actually there or not — that is if the agency continued at the same level, started to grow, or started to decline. For instance:

		Gross Income		
Year	Factor	Static Agency	Growing Agency	Declining Agency
1986	Base	$1,000,000	$1,000,000	$1,000,000
1987		1,000,000	1,125,000	875,000
1988		1,000,000	1,250,000	750,000
1989		1,000,000	1,375,000	625,000
1990		1,000,000	1,500,000	500,000
		Payment for Future Earnings		
1987	7%	$70,000	$78,750	$61,250
1988	5%	50,000	62,500	37,500
1989	3%	30,000	41,250	18,750
1990	1%	10,000	15,000	5,000
Payment for Earnings	16%	$160,000	$197,500	$122,500
Payment for Net Assets		$250,000	$250,000	$250,000
Total Cost		$410,000	$447,500	$372,500

A Phantom Premium

One final question remains: how this system could be adapted to the sale of a share of the agency to an employee and its later repurchase from him. Let's assume the employee wants to buy 10 percent of the agency and that it is in a static pattern during 1987 to 1990 when he or she is paying for the stock. The total cost would be a $25,000 down payment plus an additional $16,000 over four years for his or her share of future earning power. You collect the $25,000 down payment from him in cash but are reluctant to ask him for further cash each year for many reasons, a principal one being that, if he is a typical young agency employee, he probably doesn't have much cash to spare. So, what do you do?

Well, you tell him or her, "We'll set up this premium for future earning power on our records and call it a *phantom premium*; then when you resell the stock to the agency, we'll calculate the sale premium on the same basis and deduct from it the phantom premium so you will get the book value plus the difference in the two premiums for future earning power." If, in our example the gross income for the years during which the employee is reselling his or her stock is that shown in the second column, he would be entitled to a premium of 10 percent of $197,500 or $19,750. The actual cash receipts would be $25,000 at the time he leaves plus the net premium of $3,750 ($19,750 – $16,000). This would be paid to him as soon as the total repurchase premium exceeded the $16,000 phantom premium. At the end of the third year the total repurchase premium would be 10 percent of $182,500 or $18,250 and he would receive $2,250 in that year plus an additional $1,500 the next year.

So, to sum it all up, there is no single method or formula for valuing an agency. The two major points that must be considered are 1. the agency's net assets and 2. its future earning power. Both of these factors may have to be adjusted to reflect the realities of a particular situation and they can be combined in an almost infinite number of ways. The figures shown above are only an example, albeit a realistic one, of how to evaluate an agency. This can give you a good idea of the size of the numbers you're talking about, but the actual valuation is a problem for experts.

Different Prices for Different Buyers?

In spite of the fact you might feel that, once established on whatever basis you prefer, the value of one agency should be the same for all potential purchasers, I believe that this is not the case, nor should it be.

At one extreme is the case of an agency that wants to buy your agency for any one of a number of reasons — to get a foothold in your territory, to expand its client list, to acquire some top-notch advertising people. Whether this is called a merger as a face-saving circumlocution or is identified as the acquisition it really is, it is purely a business transaction. As such you should try to get the most advantageous deal you can.

In a transaction such as this you may use your formula valuation as a point of departure but inevitably the final price will depend on the relative bargaining power of the two parties. How anxious is the other agency to get hold of your business, your clients, and your people? How willing are you to sell out?

The factors you'll want to take into consideration will include guarantees on both sides, employment or consulting contracts, continuation of benefit programs, and terms of sale, to name a few — all highly technical areas in which you should employ expert professional advisers. Since each case is different, I'll not discuss this kind of transaction further.

At the other extreme is the situation in which an employee or group of employees may want to buy an interest in the agency where they work. These are not strangers seeking to negotiate a purely commercial deal; they are, if you will, members of the family. As such you'll probably be inclined to give them more favorable consideration and terms than you would a stranger.

Then there's an in-between group—neither competitors seeking a take-over nor present associates looking for a piece of the action—but outsiders seeking a good investment. As such they'll probably be interested primarily in investment considerations such as earnings, dividends, growth, and stability.

In the next chapter I'll discuss some of the reasons employees or others might want to buy a piece of the business and why you might want to sell to them. We'll also consider some ways in which the price might be determined for different groups.

12

Who Should Own Agency Stock?

At the end of the last chapter I talked about employees and outsiders as potential owners of agency stock. Let's now look into this whole area more closely.

Employees As Stockholders

Most agencies are started by one man or at most a small group of principals. They own all the stock though some shares may be put in their spouses' names for tax planning reasons. As the agency continues in business and, I hope, grows and prospers, it will add people, some of whom will become key employees whose activities have a definite effect on the success of the agency. At the same time the needs of the growing business may call for more capital than the present owners can, or care to, supply. So now comes the time to consider selling some stock. To whom?

Key Employees

Naturally you'll think first of your key employees. They help make the wheels go around. In earlier days they'd be taken into the firm or made a partner which is exactly what you're doing when you sell them some stock. You know them and they know you; what's probably more important is that they and your clients know each other. If all these relationships are friendly — and these guys wouldn't still be around, to say nothing of being key people, if they weren't — taking these people into the family can only strengthen the ties on which the business is based.

Why would key employees want to buy agency stock? I can think of a number of reasons.

First, stock ownership is the ultimate form of profit sharing. If a person's efforts increase the agency's profits, he or she increases the value of its stock, and the individual participates in that increase to the extent of his or her degree of ownership. Thus, to a degree, he or she is in business for him- or herself and the master of his or her own destiny.

Another benefit of stock ownership for key employees is to let them build for the future. Normally, for internal purposes, agency stock is shown at its book value, which is the smallest amount it is worth. On this basis, every time the agency earns a profit the book value goes up and every time it pays out part of its profits as a dividend the book value goes down. As employees get financial reports month after month and year after year, they can watch their nest egg grow. What's more, they know that their own activities and decisions have a direct bearing on how this nest egg grows.

Other reasons why key employees would want to own some stock in the agency for which they work would be the boost to morale on becoming "a member of the family" and the right, as a stockholder, to receive financial reports to show how the company is doing. Generally speaking, these considerations are of secondary importance to the key employees, but they do have value to them.

Middle Management
Today's middle management people may be tomorrow's key people and perhaps future owners of the agency. To prepare for these more responsible roles they should acquire some familiarity with the corporate facts of life. What better way to expose them than to let them own some stock and thus be entitled to get reports and attend stockholders' meetings to see something of what goes on behind the scenes. At the same time you'll get a chance to size them up in this milieu.

These up-and-coming youngsters will also probably get a big boost in morale from being invited to become stockholders with the recognition that status implies. If you've appraised them correctly, you'll do well to tie them closely to the agency early in their careers.

Other Employees
Sometimes stock is made available to other employees of lesser stature. Such shares usually are issued in small lots primarily to reward employees who have given the agency long and faithful service. They never can provide an important source of capital for the agency but they can give big dividends in employee morale.

Employee Trusts

Agencies that have formal pension or profit-sharing trusts qualified under the Internal Revenue Code may be able to sell (or deposit as part of an annual contribution) some of their own stock to these trusts. I know of cases where this has been done but hasten to point out that such investment requires specific approval by the Internal Revenue Service, which will be given or refused depending on the circumstances in each case.

If you can get permission for the trust to make this investment, you'll reap several benefits. First, you'll be tapping a good source of capital for your agency and, what's more, one that won't want to withdraw its money unexpectedly.

Also, every employee who is a participant in the trust will automatically have a beneficial interest in the ownership of the agency. This can be a good morale builder.

So, if you have such a trust, or are thinking about establishing one, talk to your advisers about the possibility of the trust becoming a part owner of the business. This can play a big part in your agency's future.

How to Sell Stock to Employees

When you're talking about making stock available to employees, you are, in effect, taking them into partnership. Because of this special relationship, you'll undoubtedly make it as easy as possible for them to buy in. But remember well that word "buy." Don't make the mistake of giving them stock; they'll appreciate it much more if they have to pay for it. You may give them all sorts of help but insist that they at least go through the motions of paying for the stock.

When you're thinking of selling stock to employees, your real interest is to reward outstanding performance, to tie key people more closely to the agency, to build a sound foundation for future growth. You're not trying to get the highest possible price for what you're selling. So how do you give the purchasing employee a break? Lots of ways.

Price.   As I pointed out in chapter 11, different kinds of purchasers of agency stock have different reasons for wanting to buy and you probably have different reasons for wanting to sell to each of them. Because selling stock to employees is one of the best ways to make your agency strong, you'll want to encourage employees to buy. Set the lowest price compatible with your basic valuation formula.

Payroll deductions.   Many agencies selling modest amounts of stock to employees will let them pay for it by means of payroll deductions for a reasonably short time.

Bank loans.   If the value of the stock sold is so large that realistic payroll deductions would stretch over too long a period, the agency can probably help by using its good offices to persuade its friendly banker to lend the money to the employee backed by his stock as collateral. The agency can guarantee the loan but the method I prefer, and which I have used successfully, is for the agency simply to guarantee the bank that it will repurchase any stock the bank may have to take over. In this way there's no actual or even contingent liability on the agency's books.

Bonuses.   One common device is to give the employee a bonus (which he's probably earned anyway) with the understanding that he'll use whatever of it he has left after paying taxes on the bonus to buy stock in the agency. Or you can pay the bonus in the form of stock. In this latter case you'll probably have to include some cash for the employee to use for paying the tax on the bonus.

Repurchase Agreements
When you take an associate into the firm by selling him stock, you expect he's going to be with you for a good long time. In this highly mobile business, however, he could move to greener pastures at almost any time.

You certainly don't want an employee who leaves you for a competitor to continue to be one of the owners of your business. So, have a formal stock repurchase agreement that you have everyone sign when first becoming a stockholder. This should leave nothing to chance but should set forth explicitly the conditions under which you can get hold of the stock, the price to be paid for it, and other matters of this sort.

As to price, some agreements call for one price if a man quits, another if he gets fired, and still another if he retires or dies. Some even go so far as to repurchase it under some conditions at exactly what the employee paid for it. While there may be many reasons why you'd want to have an agreement of this kind, I think the fairest way for everyone—and hence for the agency in the long run—is to use the same basis for buying back as you used when you sold the stock. That is, if you sold it at book value, buy it back at its present book value; if you used a formula related to gross income when selling the stock, use the same formula (with the numbers updated) when you buy it back.

Outside Stockholders
Once you get away from selling stock to your associates in the agency you're bound to run up against a whole new set of values and priorities. Your

business associates are advertising professionals who know how hazardous the agency business is, how slim its operating margins are, how dependent it is on the intangibles of personal skills and accumulated specialized experience, how often accounts are lost as a result of someone's whim with no real fault on the part of the agency. They accept all this as an integral part of the business and, if they're really dedicated to their careers, want to be part owners of the business in spite of uncertainties and risks. They feel that their personal skills and contributions will go a long way toward overcoming the problems and making them masters of their own destiny.

Excluding an occasional rich uncle who wants to help you out, the only two groups of nonemployees who might be interested in buying agency stock are some of the agency's clients and the general public. Because the reasons for their wanting to buy and your wanting to sell are different in each case, let's look at them separately.

Clients

Other than getting money that may be needed to increase working capital, why would you consider a client as a purchaser of some of your agency's stock? One reason certainly might be to cement more tightly the agency-client relationship. After all, a client is a lot less likely to fire an agency of which he owns a piece.

Another reason might be a feeling on your part that you'd be doing business with a friend, quite possibly one of long-standing, who knows something of the agency business and its rapid changes. As such, he'd probably be much less likely to make waves if things slipped a little once in a while. He might even make his purchase of your stock on more favorable terms than a complete stranger would offer.

Why would the client be interested in buying your stock? He may be buying it purely for its investment value, but that's not likely to be his principal reason. He's more apt to want to strengthen the agency-client relationship from his side so you won't be tempted to go after the account of one of his competitors. He may think he'll save some money by getting favored treatment from you or, at least, getting back some of his advertising expenditures by way of dividends on your stock.

"So," you may say, "there seem to be some pretty good reasons on both sides. Should we seriously consider letting a client become a stockholder?" My answer must be a resounding "no!" for this is starting on the road to becoming a house agency.

Becoming a House Agency

The October 1986 issue of the *Standard Directory of Advertising Agencies* lists 3,562 U.S. agencies, of which 107 frankly identify themselves as house agencies. Some of these claim billings of up to $60 million. There are undoubtedly many more that can't readily be identified, but these are pretty impressive figures. So what's so bad about being a house agency? I think there's a lot wrong with house agencies from the viewpoint of the agency and the advertiser.

Let's look at it from the agency's point of view first. The minute an agency changes into a house agency, you as one of its principals stop working for yourself and become a mere employee. You're no longer master of your own fate. You can't take a flyer which, if successful, could be a gold mine for you but which would hurt no one but you if it flops. You've lost the profit motive.

On the creative side there would be none of the stimulus that comes from the cross-fertilization of ideas with people who are working in completely different areas. You'd miss the thrilling exposure to new advertising techniques devised originally for an industrial product, but which, with a little imagination, can be adapted to consumer products.

You'd lose the continuous exposure to a broad range of problems and hence, in time, a large part of your objectivity and even professionalism. You're bound to start losing your broad outlook and narrowing your horizons. Pretty soon you might be in danger of not being able to see the forest for the trees.

How about the advertiser who has his own house agency? After a while his advertising is bound to suffer from these same narrowing horizons and lack of cross-fertilization of ideas. His agency staff is always in danger of going stale with predictable and unfortunate results on advertising quality. If he becomes unhappy with a regular independent full-service agency, in the last resort he can fire that agency and hire a new one; this is almost impossible with a house agency.

The independent agency with a number of different clients can afford to keep a large staff with highly diversified skills because it can shift their efforts from a temporarily slack account to one that's at its peak of activity. It can call on the unique skills of an artist to solve a problem that may not come up again for a year for a particular client. Because that artist's skills are regularly in demand by a diversified list of clients, the agency can keep him busy as a key member of the staff. A house agency, with a single client, can't always do this.

Finally, how about the argument most often advanced for using a house agency, namely that the client will be able to keep for itself the profit the agency normally would make. I think this is a pretty weak argument because I doubt that the house agency can operate as efficiently as the independent agency with a much broader base of clients and products over which to spread its activities and its costs. Even assuming, for the sake of argument, equally efficient operation, the profit to be expected on an advertising expenditure of $1 million is only $83,000. This seems a very small amount for which to risk the success of the $1 million expenditure by using less than the most professional advertising people available.

Going Public

In recent years there has been a great deal of interest in agencies going public by offering some of their shares to the general public. As a matter of fact the first such offering was made in October 1929 by Albert Frank-Guenther Law, which sold a very small percentage of its shares. There was no further activity towards going public until September 1962 when Papert, Koenig, Lois sold about 20 percent of its shares to the public. Since then some 25 or 30 other agencies have followed the same course; interestingly enough, four have reversed themselves and gone private again.

Benefits for the agency?   Why would an agency want to sell stock to the public? There are many reasons but the principal one has to be money. If you look into the public offerings you'll see that in almost every case the great bulk of the stock offered to the public has been sold by agency principals and not by the corporation. As a matter of fact, out of the public offerings for which data is available in *Standard & Poor's* or *Moody's*, 78.5 percent of the shares sold were for the account of stockholders and only 21.5 percent for the benefit of the agency itself. So, the motivation would seem to be to let the principal owners withdraw some of their investment in the agency. This is fine for the owners but does nothing for the agency itself.

There are expectations that going public will redound to the benefit of the agency. Its liquidity might be enhanced by having its stock marketable; it might be easier to make desirable acquisitions if a publicly held stock can be offered.

Having its stock publicly traded might constitute recognition of the agency as being in the top ranks of the business and the attendant publicity could bring the agency new business.

For the agency's employees, these same factors could be expected to increase morale and offer an incentive to greater effort. Their stake in the agency would be liquid and hence of greater value.

I have no way of knowing, of course, how these expectations worked out in practice for all the agencies involved. I can get some insight into the problems encountered from an article in *Advertising Age* (Sept. 3, 1973, p. 1) in which Clint Frank was quoted as saying that his agency had not received any of the expected benefits from public ownership. On the contrary, the decline in the stock's quoted value in spite of "hard work, good service and even reasonable profits" had had a damaging effect on the morale of employee investors who saw the value of their investment in the agency dwindling. So, the Clinton E. Frank agency went private again.

What the public wants.   Why would members of the general public be interested in buying the stock of advertising agencies? Presumably for the same reasons they would make any investment. The yardsticks by which they would evaluate any company investment are, in approximate order of importance, 1. management efficiency and ability, 2. financial stability, 3. earnings and dividends, 4. the relationship between assets and liabilities, and 5. capital structure. Simply by listing these we see how different the agency business is from most others. Let's examine each of them.

Of course, able management is important to an advertising agency, but in evaluating it bear in mind that what makes an agency really tick is the quality of its creative product. This is not something that management can plan for as it can, for example, predict demand for a smaller automobile that it then proceeds to manufacture. Successful management in the agency business is the one that so manages its people and the conditions under which they work that the creative juices flow freely and the agency produces great advertising. This kind of management is hard to evaluate unless you are working in the agency day in and day out.

As for financial stability, the largest agencies probably have it to a reasonable degree, but even they are subject to the vicissitudes of the business and the whims of clients. All you have to do is to read in *Advertising Age* each year the list of major account changes. In 1976 these amounted to $576.5 million which increased in 1981 to $1.4 billion. While the complete record for 1986 has not yet been compiled in the months of April and May alone, following the "megamergers" of Saatchi & Saatchi and Bates and the formation of Omnicom from BBDO, Doyle Dane Bernbach, and Needham, Harper & Steers, these account shifts were made: Saatchi/Bates lost $255 million net; Omnicon lost $117 million net while nonmerging Young & Rubicam gained $254 million net.

That ain't hay, even for the biggest agencies! What's probably even more disturbing to the general investing public is the high degree of publicity regularly given these shifts of accounts between agencies. Many metropolitan newspapers run advertising columns that regularly list changes of accounts and also the comings and goings of key agency personnel.

I've talked before, particularly in chapter 6, about the ability of the owners of an advertising agency to shift their own compensation, within rather broad limits, between salary, bonus, dividends, and appreciation in the value of their holdings of agency stock. This capability also extends to planning deliberately for zero profit in a given year to allow yourself to do other things—such as give extra rewards to key people—which will be much more beneficial to the agency in the long run.

As soon as you put stock in the hands of the public you're bound to lose some of your freedom of action. Your outside stockholders will expect earnings and dividends regularly and won't appreciate that it may be in their best interest to forego earnings and dividends once in a while. As a matter of fact it's interesting to note that the president of one of the formerly publicly owned agencies, now in private ownership again, gave as one of the reasons for withdrawing from public ownership, the fact that he wanted to run the agency for the benefit of its employees rather than the stockholders.

As for assets and liabilities, an agency has no bricks and mortar, no machinery and equipment of any consequence, no patents, no valuable ownership of rights, no carefully constructed distribution system, no long-term contracts, and no exclusive privileges. Its only real assets — creativity, ideas, and talent — can't possibly be translated into balance sheet terms. On the contrary, most agencies operate in leased offices and have their names on long-term noncancellable leases that over a period of five years can add up to something approaching half their capital.

Under present accounting procedures these leases appear as notes to the financial statements and not as liabilities on the balance sheet. They could, however, pose a serious problem if things start to go bad.

Finally, capitalization. As I've pointed out, an agency is a people-intensive business rather than a capital-intensive one like a steel mill. This means that the amount of capital available for sale to the public is limited by the nature of the business. It's further limited by the desire of the principals to control the agency and thus their own destiny. A study of public offerings shows that, on the average, only 30 percent of an agency's shares were offered to the public and in no case as much as 43 percent. So, the public is bound to be a perpetual minority stockholder.

How have agency stocks performed? How have they treated the members of the investing public that have bought them? Let's look at the record. From standard published sources I've compared the price of each of five publicly owned agency stocks at their high and low points for 10 years and compared this with the *Standard & Poor's 500 Index*. These are the results:

Stock	High as % of Low	Final Year High as % of First Year Low
Foote, Cone & Belding	144.0%	472.0%
Interpublic Group	163.3	762.5
JWT Group	158.4	619.4
Ogilvy Group	149.3	823.5
Omnicom	158.5	483.1
Standard & Poor's 500 Index	126.4	280.0

Another measure of the increasing acceptance by the public of agency stocks is shown by the fact that in the same 10-year period the average price/earnings ratio for the agency stocks has gone up from 5.76 to 15.80 as follows:

Year	P/E
1977	5.94
1978	6.42
1979	5.86
1980	7.28
1981	10.18
1982	11.18
1983	13.74
1984	10.66
1985	14.92
1986	15.80

Both of these tests show that agency stocks, while not top-grade blue chips, are very acceptable performers.

Summary. So, I must conclude that going public is a good device for the agency principal who, for whatever reason, wants to get all or part of his money out of the agency. It may have some benefits for the agency, but I think they are marginal at best and may be vastly outweighed by the erosion of employee morale and agency image if the stock declines in price in the face of what the agency people know to be highly successful operations.

I also can't help feeling that, while agency stock ownership is a tremendous benefit and incentive for agency employees, it is a reasonable investment for the general public so long as they stick to the size and quality of agencies listed above. For other, smaller agencies with a much more limited market, investment in agency stock is not recommended to the general public.

Perhaps the most important aspect of this whole question of outside participation in agency ownership is the effect it may have on what we now call "our public image."

We who are in the business know how hazardous it is. We know from sad experience that through no fault of our own we lose accounts we deserve. We know how narrow is our margin of operations, how difficult it is to show a profit. We're willing to take a chance, to work hard, and be so valuable to our clients that they will stay with us. Often this policy pays off. But suppose it doesn't and we have to explain matters to outsiders who have invested their money. Will they understand? You know that, as in any business, the many are condemned because of the failures or misbehavior of the few. What if we add a money loss to their supply of brickbats?

Think twice before you sell stock in your agencies to outsiders. The main objection, as I see it, is the possibility of endangering our business standing, our priceless reputation for integrity. The risks we rightly take in our own shops can boomerang with fatal results if we let outsiders take them too. This prospect is bad medicine for our business.

=13=

How Can You
Transfer Ownership?

Being natural optimists, the principals of advertising agencies expect that they'll live forever and see no point in thinking now about transferring the ownership and management of their agency to other hands at some time in the dim dark future.

The folly of this attitude can be demonstrated by the case of the medium-sized agency owned by men I'll call simply John and Bill. This is a true story and I know the people involved but won't divulge names to prevent embarrassment. John and Bill each owned half of the agency and everything was running smoothly until one afternoon Bill dropped dead in his office. Just like that!

The agency's treasury bought Bill's stock from his estate and John became sole owner. This transaction went smoothly and all seemed well. Then John began to worry about his health, even to the point of believing he was in imminent danger of dying. For the first time he wondered, "Who's going to buy my stock? If we handle it the way we did Bill's, it'll take the agency's entire capital and there won't be that much cash anyway." He concluded he had only two choices—either liquidate the agency or seek an outside buyer. He chose the latter alternative, but his bargaining position was such that he got much less than he might have under better controlled conditions. How do you avoid this?

Plan Ahead Now

If you're willing to restrict yourself to the two choices with which John was faced, little planning is needed. If you go along with simple liquidation of the agency, all you need do is see that the assets are as liquid as possible and that they represent real and not wishful values.

The other option, sale to another agency, doesn't need much planning either. You'll undoubtedly get a more favorable deal if you sell your agency at a time when you can offer your personal active involvement for some period after the sale. This option calls for some planning, at least to the point where you set about doing it before illness or death forces someone else to do it for you.

The third option — and the one I believe most agency principals will want to adopt — is to have your agency continue operations, but under new management. This does require a lot of advance planning. The basic questions for which you're going to need answers are: 1. to whom should management responsibilities and control be transferred, 2. how and when should the transfer be accomplished, and 3. what device can be helpful in achieving this transfer?

Who Should Take Over?

Obviously the ideal purchasers are the people who can carry on the affairs of the agency with the least disruption and the greatest possibility of success. This means, of course, your present associates in the agency. They know the clients and their needs; they know the principles and philosophy on which the agency has been operating; they've devoted time and talent and effort to the agency; they've earned the chance to take over.

The key people in the agency, account executives and department heads, certainly should be included in the new ownership. If you believe, as I do, that a share in the ownership of an agency is one of the best and most widely appreciated ways of rewarding contributions to the agency's success, at the same time tying good people more closely to the agency, you'll want to consider extending the benefits of ownership beyond the key employee group.

Certainly consider the middle management group. They're likely to be the next generation of key employees and by considering them now you'll be one jump ahead in planning for a future change of management. With the whole group — present key people and potential key people — consider apportioning shares in the ownership of the agency in relation to their contributions to its success. If you're foresighted you'll include some present evaluation of the future contributions of the junior members of the group.

How Do You Transfer Ownership?

Since most agencies are organized as corporations, the transfer of any part of the ownership is accomplished by the sale of shares of stock. So, what's complicated about that? Nothing until you come face to face with the fact that most agency people don't have a lot of ready cash with which to buy stock. What's needed is a stock purchase plan to allow employees to buy stock on terms they can afford. Here are some methods for achieving this.

Payroll Purchase Plan

With this arrangement, you tell the employee who's buying stock that you'll accept payment over a period of months by making regular deductions from his or her paychecks. Of course you must have a cash down payment from him or her and you'll need a signed agreement to cover the monthly deductions. This kind of plan puts you in the banking business, which is not your forte, so you'll want to put pretty strict limits on how far you go. Generally, I think any payments for stock purchased under a payroll deduction plan should be completed within a year.

Bank Loan Plan

If the amount involved in the purchase of a block of stock is larger than you can conveniently handle, or want to, on a payroll deduction basis, consider working out with your banker a program under which he'll advance the necessary funds. Of course, he'll probably want some assurance from you before making the loan.

You could guarantee the loan to the bank or even co-sign the note, but this puts at least contingent liabilities on your books that you may not want. Another way is to tell the banker that if he accepts your agency's stock as collateral for the loan to the employee—which he would do anyway—the agency will guarantee to buy from the bank any shares it may have to take over in case of default. In this way, you're really utilizing the agency's credit to help the employees buy stock, but as long as everything goes as you hope it will, no liability appears on the agency's books.

Low Priced Stock

Another device some agencies have used is to create a second class of stock. This new stock has a very low value, but at the proper time it can be given control of the agency by converting the original stock, which the principals continue to own, into a preferred stock to be retired out of earnings on some mutually agreeable basis. There are many ways of doing this, including the use of a voting trust, but the details can get pretty complicated; so be sure to consult expert advisers before starting on a program like this.

ESOP

This acronym stands for Employee Stock Ownership Plan and represents a device that recently gained attention after lying dormant in the tax structure for many years.

This kind of trust is a variation of the stock bonus trust that was first recognized in the tax code in 1921. Little was heard of it, however, until it received special recognition and favorable tax treatment in a series of tax laws enacted in 1973–75.

Basically, an ESOP is a trust, qualified under the Internal Revenue Code, whose principal purpose is to use before-tax dollars contributed to the trust by the agency for the purpose of buying agency stock for later distribution to employees. The stock can be purchased from retiring principal owners or from the agency's treasury. This lets the ESOP become a device for transferring agency ownership from retiring principals to second generation management or it can be used to raise additional capital to finance agency growth.

Like everything else an ESOP is not the answer to every agency's problems under all circumstances. There are limitations and conditions surrounding its use that may make it undesirable for many agencies. But, in the right circumstances, it can be a lifesaver.

When you're talking with your expert advisers — accountants, lawyers, and bankers, to name just a few — about plans for raising capital or for the eventual transfer of ownership of the agency, by all means ask them to look into an ESOP and its application to your particular circumstances. This particular device has been given even greater tax advantages under the 1986 Tax Reform Law.

Other Things to Consider in Your Plan

Once you've decided on a basic plan you'll want to look into some features that may be helpful in some cases.

Buy-Sell Agreement
If the agency is owned by a small group of principals, it would be wise to work out between them a buy-sell agreement. This would set forth just what happens to the stock of each principal if he or she should die, retire, or simply leave the agency. You'll want to be specific about whether the agency or the other principals buy(s) the stock. Be sure to establish how the price is to be set and how the stock is to be apportioned among the purchasers. You can make any provisions you want, but the important thing is to work the program out well in advance.

Insurance
Many agencies use life insurance on the principals as a means of funding a buy-sell agreement. These policies can be owned and the premiums paid

by the agency itself or by the other principals. Of course, every case is different, but it's certainly something you'll want to look into; and don't forget the tax consequences of the different ways of handling the insurance.

Consultation Contracts

Many, if not most, principals won't want to cut all ties to the agency when they retire. The agency probably wouldn't want that either, nor the clients who've been relying on the retiree's advice for many years. One way to ease the transition is to write a contract for consultation by the retiring principal so you can call on him as needed in future years. This keeps him interested, gives the agency the benefit of his experience, and can go a long way towards solving the financial problems that can arise for both agency and principal at retirement time.

Gradual Phasing Out

One plan I've seen in operation calls for a gradual progression towards full retirement, beginning five years before the anticipated retirement date. During the first year, the principal sells a fifth of his stock in the agency and takes a two-month vacation; the second year he sells another fifth of his stock and increases his vacation to three months. This goes on until, at the end of the fifth year, all his stock has been redeemed and he has gradually increased his time off to such an extent that it's but a short step to full retirement. During the five-year period it would be quite reasonable to make reductions in salary as vacation time increases.

This kind of plan has the advantage for the retiring principal of making a gradual shift from full participation to none, as regards agency ownership, working time, and income. For the agency it has the advantage of knowing when stock is to be repurchased, and how much, and being able to plan to meet the changes in personnel requirements. It seems to me to make more sense than to go serenely on until retirement day and then whammo.

Summary

The one point I want to drive home is this: plan *now* for the transfer of ownership to avoid real problems when the time comes, and when, realistically, you may not be around to help work them out. The specific steps I described briefly are only a few of the approaches you'll want to think about.

Every situation is different — different people, clients, financial situation, business climate, and desires on the part of the principals. These specifics were mentioned only to give you a basis for your own thinking and discussion with your advisers. It's important to remember that with plans as complicated as these you must have the best professional advice you can get. This is no field for do-it-yourself projects. The point is, each of these devices has worked, and worked well, for one agency or another. Maybe one of them is just what you want.

But plan ahead! Don't wait! Do it today!

IV Agency Organization and Operations

=14===

People—Your Most Important Asset

Probably there never was a business so highly personal as advertising. It depends for success on individual work, inspiration, and enthusiasm. It makes use of temperamental, imaginative, highly strung individuals to whom a word of praise in the proper spot can mean far more than money. So the selection, training, and handling of your people is about the most important thing you can do to insure success.

How Do You Locate and Select People?

How do you pick those rare individuals who can help an agency for the long range. For example, an agency is expanding and needs additional personnel. It defines its requirements precisely; it probes the applicants' samples and checks their references; it uses psychological tests, but with only moderate success. Apart from all these methods for finding good employees, are there any additional techniques or approaches?

From the reference to samples, the agency is apparently seeking to fill a creative job, but the general principles to be used in recruiting for any job are the same. The differences between selecting people to fill one job or another will be basically differences in the emphasis given one factor or another.

What Are You Really Looking for?

First, it is advisable to define clearly the kind of people you want in your agency, all the way down the line, and refuse to hire anyone who does not meet these specifications. You want honesty, loyalty, balance, humanity, realism, the willingness to work, and the refusal to feel that "the world owes me a living." Write your own ticket, but make it good.

Second, set down in full detail the responsibilities of the job you are seeking to fill. In the case of the creative person apparently being sought in the above example, just what is expected and on what terms? Do you want independent writers and planners or people who work best in creative groups or under the guidance of a copy chief? Must they do contact in addition to their creative duties? In brief, just exactly what is the job?

Third, add to your list of basic traits you seek in all employees some others that would be particularly applicable to the specific job you are filling. These might include ability, knowledge, and experience, all of them defined in terms of the specific job. You'll notice that experience is listed last. This is done deliberately because, while a track record is desirable, even if a person hasn't had much experience it will be acquired fast, provided the other essentials are present.

What Do You Have to Offer?

Before seeking new people, you should look carefully at your own situation. What makes your shop a desirable place to work? Why should any able advertising man or woman prefer your agency, compared with others offering practically the same money? Without this plus, you will have difficulty in attracting the type of people you want—ambitious, able, and loyal. Set your standards high, but to attract this sort of personnel you must come out on top when rated by these same standards yourself.

So, let's see what qualifications make an agency a good place to work.

Realistically, money is the first consideration. Not necessarily only the amount, but also the manner of earning and receiving. While good advertising people will not want to make financial sacrifices to join an agency, they will be favorably inclined towards any agency that makes them feel they deserve the money they get and their remuneration bears a direct relationship to the money the agency is making on them. This brings us to the ways of rewarding people, which will be discussed in a later section of this chapter.

The second element that makes an agency a good place to work is appreciation. Creative people particularly need this. They simply cannot work efficiently and happily without being patted on the back when they deserve it. As an agency owner planning to take on creative personnel you must look at yourself sharply and realistically. How good an employer are you? How well can you understand and sympathize with the idiosyncracies of others? Are you tolerant? Are you kind? Or are you a martinet, using fear instead of constructive and helpful comments? Just because you are successful yourself, and above average in your abilities, can you appreciate the efforts of others who are perhaps less well endowed? When an individual falls down on a job, is your first instinct to fire him or do you wonder if he would do better work in some other capacity?

Returning to the original inquiry of this section, the answer may well be, "If you want people of the high caliber you outline, it is not enough to put them through all the fitness tests. Subject yourself to the same analysis, or one even more rigorous. How well have you held on to your present personnel? How long have good people stayed with you? When you lost some, was it your fault or theirs?

A great responsibility rests on any employer who has in his hands the happiness and peace of mind of even a few employees. He has no right to hope they are happy. It is his duty to see that they are, because his is a position of power. Tranquility or fear? Which do you hand out? Answer this correctly, and you will have solved the major problem of better associates.

Where Do You Look for People?

Well, of course, you have access to all the regular sources such as employment agencies. There are even some of these, mainly in New York and Chicago, that specialize in advertising people. Then there are the classified ads in newspapers and in the advertising press — *Advertising Age* and regional publications. Another resource is your local Ad Club. Most cities of any size have an Ad Club and often an Art Directors Club or other specialized groups. If you belong to an agency network, the executive secretary may know of available people. Other possible sources are the many colleges that offer courses in advertising. Most of them keep lists of their graduates and many stand ready to help them find the kind of jobs they want. Make contact with the deans of these schools.

The agency business is a volatile one because advertisers change agencies with often distressing frequency, agency people shift from one shop to another, and agencies merge or, on occasion, split apart. What's more, all this is made highly visible by regular listing of such changes in the national and regional advertising publications, the daily advertising columns that appear in many metropolitan newspapers, and in bulletins from the *Standard Directory of Advertising Agencies*.

From all these published sources you may get a pretty good idea of available people. Let me be very clear about this: I am not advocating piracy of other agencies' staffs. Most agency principals, however, when faced with the necessity of reducing staff because of lost accounts or mergers are eager to help their people find new jobs. So, inquire around and you may help them while helping yourself.

Educating Your People

Questions on how much agency people should know, before and after being hired, how to pick the right men and women and then make them better, how much time can profitably be spent on education compared with that used in the more obvious agency activities are much more important than they seem on the surface.

Too often sight is lost of the fact that a business depending on the abilities of individuals, glibly called a service business, must give better and better service to survive. It's not enough to worry about the end product of marketing and advertising advice and its implementation in the form of plans and copy. Agencies succeed in direct proportion to the abilities of their people.

So it would be well, I think, if agency heads wondered occasionally if continuing attention to education such as the medical professions demand might not be advisable and profitable for our business.

What is the too-frequent agency image of today, as seen by the advertisers? Cleverness, the ability to make a fast buck, superficiality, irresponsibility? Wouldn't agencies be better off if they were thought of as staffed by responsible, well-educated, soundly based individuals who think before they speak, look before they leap? Certainly if agencies want the latter image, they need the personnel to build better agencies. They need educated people who know that education never stops, and it's our responsibility to help them continue learning all through their business lives.

One East Coast agency I know took an unusual approach to this problem. It set up an internship program that recruited students from local colleges to work in the agency under the dual supervision of the agency's account executives and the college faculty. They work as a team with overall responsibility for research, creative ideas, media placement, mechanicals, and other such duties. The first group of three, a writer, a graphics designer, and a writer/producer, got straight As for enthusiasm, effort, and performance. When the program ended the graphics designer became a permanent member of the agency staff, one of the others went to a New York agency, and the third set about writing plays. The agency considers the experiment a success.

Once you've found and employed the kind of desirable people you're seeking, you should begin to educate them in agency techniques and procedures and keep on doing so. Instead of letting your people spend their time adding up figures, clipping tear sheets, writing to someone else's specifications, drawing along preprinted lines, see that they know why they are doing what they are doing, and what it means in the final agency product.

This can be done by swapping jobs occasionally, by frequent get-togethers of all of the agency employees to discuss their own output and that of others, and by some sort of review by the bosses at reasonable intervals to see what they're learning.

Work hard and constantly, you agency owners and managers, to sell your people on the need to know more, to be of greater potential value to your clients. Resist the notion that new ideas are better than good ideas. Get the whole shop sold on the theory that we are in a reputable business, that our customers trust us to advise them soundly, that we succeed only as we help our clients succeed, along sound and constructive lines. Discourage opportunism, snap judgments, and fast footwork. Encourage honesty, hard work, letting the chips fall where they may, and giving the other fellow his money's worth.

Don't expect your people to stay overtime to be educated. Teach them on company time, not on theirs.

To summarize: Get the right people with the right educational background. Keep on educating them by practical experience, case histories, and talks by executives who know what they are talking about. Hang plenty of carrots in front of their noses in the way of incentives and recognition for achievement.

When you, or your people—or any of us for that matter—stop learning, we are on the way out.

How Do You Compensate Your People?

"Simple," you say, "you pay them." Well of course that's true, but that's not the whole story because there are many ways of paying people. Also, different kinds of compensation may have more or less appeal for different people depending on their age, health, family status, and other considerations. What appeals most to Joe today may be a lot less attractive a few years from now after his kids are educated and he begins to consider the possibility of retirement. So let's look at the different forms compensation can take.

Salary
Salary, of course, is the largest single part of an employee's compensation. When it's paid will be determined by local custom in your market. In some cities a weekly payroll is the accepted practice while in others semimonthly is the most common.

While the timing of salary payments is automatic the amount of the salary is anything but. The basic consideration in setting an employee's salary must be what he or she is contributing to each of the functions the agency must perform. The guidelines given in chapter 5 can be a real help in the evaluation of responsibilities. To show how this can work, let's assume that Joe Blow, an account executive, is responsible for two accounts that together bring in $200,000 out of the $1 million of total agency income. The amounts available for salaries for the various functions might look like this:

Client	ABC	XYZ
Gross Income	$120,000	$80,000
Contact (approximately 19%)	22,800	15,200
Creative (approximately 16%)	19,200	12,800
Implemental (approximately 11%)	13,200	8,800

In addition, 11 percent of the $1 million total agency income would be allotted to general administration and new business. That is $110,000.

Let's also assume that Joe does 75 percent of the contact on ABC and 50 percent of the XYZ contact; 20 percent of ABC creative; 17 percent of XYZ implemental (he buys the media); and 10 percent of the agency's administration and new business.

This can be put together to give us a rough approximation of what the agency can afford to pay for the things Joe does.

Contact	75% of ABC	$17,100	
	50% of XYZ	7,600	$24,700
Creative	20% of ABC		3,840
Implemental	17% of XYZ		1,496
General and Admin.	10% of Total		11,000
			$41,036

So, as a point of departure in considering Joe's salary you would be in the area of $41,000. This should be checked against the going rates in your city and especially those paid by local agencies comparable to yours. You can't afford to get too far out of line.

Another important consideration is what salary Joe feels he would need to make him a happy, productive member of your team. If you feel he has real potential to become, in time, a part owner of your agency you may want to go a little higher to hold him. When talking compensation with people of high caliber and promise, be sure to discuss the whole compensation picture with them—not salary alone, but other benefits, especially profit sharing and possible future participation in the ownership of the business.

Salary or Commission?

You may well ask, "If you can come up with an approximate salary for an account executive by applying your basic guideline percentages, why not go all the way and pay him totally by a commission based on these guidelines?"

You can do this, of course, and many agencies do. Arrangements for a split of gross income between agency and account executive are fairly common.

For many reasons I don't like this way of compensating account executives. On purely philosophical grounds I dislike the implication that the accounts a person handles are his or her accounts and he or she is simply using the agency's supporting services. This may be true, at least initially, but to accept this premise puts the agency in a vulnerable position. If the accounts really belong to this person, he or she can take them and go elsewhere whenever he or she wants, which does the agency no good at all.

I think you should adopt the far better philosophy that all accounts are *agency* accounts—and then do everything you can to make that a reality. Make sure the client sees more agency people than just the account executive; make sure he or she is aware of the contributions made by all of your people.

On a more practical note, you can't run an agency by feeding numbers into a computer. The percentages I've been talking about are very useful as guidelines, but that's all they are. Every agency is different, so adjustments always have to be made; what's more the situation in any single agency is continually changing and what may be true today may be dead wrong six months from now.

Another practical problem is that these guidelines are designed to cover functions, so if a man needs help in contacting his client, the cost of that help has to come out of the percentage of income allotted to the contact function. You can't dock a man's income just because the boss goes along on a few client calls, and you surely can't tell the boss he can't go. But the value of the boss' time must come out of the contact allotment. So, you can see how this system will probably result in questions about who's doing what on an account, how much he's doing, and whether it's really necessary.

About all that can be said in favor of this way of paying account executives is that it is better than remuneration based solely on comparative bargaining power. At least it has some foundation in fact and is a formula an agency can follow with assurance of not going broke.

Reward for New Business?

Isn't it fairly common to reward an employee who brings in a new account by paying him or her a commission based on the gross income from the new account? Yes, it is, but I feel it's subject to all the objections discussed above. There's also the added complication of deciding who is really responsible for getting a new account. It's very rare that only one person can be credited with bringing in a new account. What if the boss goes along for the presentation?

If you can get around the problem of who is entitled to what part of the credit for landing a new account, some financial reward may be appropriate. This could be a percentage of the income generated, but if you follow this route, be sure to put a time limit on it—say one year. Or you can make a single lump sum payment with the amount set in reasonable relation to the size of the account.

I believe, however, that the best way to reward a man's contribution to new business is to make the results of that activity one of the things you consider when you're making a periodic review of his total progress. Thus, new business activities can, and should, be an important part of an overall evaluation and salary adjustment.

How About Bonuses?

There are two kinds of bonus that are widely used. One is the year-end bonus, usually a relatively small amount distributed to all employees on a uniform formula as a sort of Christmas present. There's no real problem here except that you should keep reminding your people that this is a bonus and not part of their regular salary. If you don't do this, you may have a full-scale crisis on your hands in a bad year when you can't make any extra payment.

The other kind of bonus is the purely discretionary one used to reward selected people for outstanding individual performances. The thing to watch out for here is that payment of such bonuses may become a habit—and an expanding habit at that—that employees come to expect. So, make it truly a reward for unusually valuable individual performance. Don't distribute such bonuses to most of your staff but single out the top performers. Don't pay bonuses to the same man year after year; if he's that consistently an outstanding performer, his salary should be adjusted.

Pensions and Profit-Sharing

These are the two most common forms of retirement plans. As such they are an important part of your total compensation package. While there are any number of informal plans called by one or the other of these names, what I'm writing about here are formal plans approved by Internal Revenue and designed to provide deferred benefits for the participants. It is a feature of all these plans that payments into them are not taxable when they are made, but only later when withdrawals start.

In return for these tax benefits, Internal Revenue has set up very strict rules and regulations as to what you can and can't do. Since the rules are changed from time to time it is very important that you consult your attorney and your auditor before establishing one of these plans or making any changes in an existing plan.

The fundamental difference between the two types of plan is that the pension plan provides fixed dollar benefits and imposes fixed costs on the agency which must be paid whether the agency earns a profit or not. It is basically an actuarial proposition, that is, a strictly mathematical calculation based on age, length of service, and salary.

The profit-sharing plan, on the other hand, provides a proportionate share in the total fund that has been built up. There's no compulsion on the agency to make a contribution unless it has profits to share. The agency's contribution can be based on a formula or it can be largely discretionary. Such a plan won't become a burdensome obligation in a poor year and will let you make up for lost time in a good year.

A sound profit-sharing plan should let employees participate on a basis that recognizes their length of service and the value of their contribution as measured by their salaries. Any number of systems using points to measure these two factors can be used to tailor a plan to your own shop and its people within reasonable limits. You might, for example, give one point for each year of service and one point for each $100 of annual salary. Or you can change the point schedule to give more weight to either service or salary as befits your particular situation.

I am a wholehearted advocate of profit-sharing as a vital part in an agency's plan for compensating its people. Its growth from year to year lets a key employee see some direct results from his or her own efforts on behalf of the agency.

Share in Ownership
To invite a key employee who's shown the ability and loyalty to become a part owner of the business is the ultimate degree of profit sharing. But it's a lot more than that. It's making your employee a member of the family; it's saying loud and clear for all to hear, "Here's a person in whom we have confidence and who is going places." It takes him out of the employee category and transforms him into one of the bosses—a person who's in business for himself.

I talked in chapter 12 about how you go about sharing your ownership. Go back and reread it!

Fringe Benefits
This category covers a large group of programs an agency may offer to some or all of its people. One of the most common is an insurance package that may include any or all kinds of protection for the employee—life insurance

on him- or herself, hospital and medical protection for him or her and family members, disability income insurance, and other new coverages that are being dreamed up all of the time. This kind of insurance usually is bought on a group basis at a more favorable rate than the employee could obtain individually. The agency may pay the whole cost or share it with the employee.

Some agencies, if business needs warrant, may make automobiles or club memberships or the use of recreational facilities like fishing lodges available to some employees. Some agencies have been known to lend a valued employee part of the down payment on a house or arrange bank credit for him or her.

Fringe benefits will appeal differently to every employee. The agency that uses them imaginatively and tries to tailor them to individual cases will be rewarded by increased employee loyalty and morale, and reduced turnover.

Holding on to Your People

Agency people are of more than average intelligence and drive; they're usually creative, pretty highly strung, somewhat emotional, and certainly sensitive. You have only to look at any issue of *Advertising Age* to know that they're highly mobile. Sometimes they're lured by the glamour of one of the major advertising centers, sometimes by what seem to be greener pastures in a competing agency in your own city. So, how do you hold on to a good employee in whom you have a large investment of time and money?

By Proper Treatment

Failure on the part of the boss to treat his account executives properly is probably the cause of most break-ups. It usually results from the power that inherently belongs to the agency head, for no doubt about it, power is one of the most difficult things for humans to handle. Unless you are acutely aware of this, unless you sense the fear and uncertainty that besets the person you've hired, and whom you can fire if you feel like it, you're looking for trouble.

The proper procedure obviously is to put yourself in the shoes of the individual concerned. Ask yourself how you would feel if you were in the job, being handled as this person is now being handled. Don't fool yourself by thinking, "He's not as sensitive as I would be," or "He's had a lot easier time than I had."

Whether you are motivated by a genuine desire to do justice to another human being or because you have sense enough to realize you can't hold him unless you do, lean over backwards to make your key employees happier and more prosperous than they would be in a business of their own. Truth and justice are powerful medicines for the ailments so often encountered in human relations.

By Adequate Compensation

No doubt about it, people are held best by a proper remuneration program properly administered. This covers all the forms of compensation discussed earlier in this chapter. An adequate salary is probably the strongest single tie binding your people to your agency in almost all cases. So make sure that your salary levels are competitive.

In other cases, however, salary alone is not enough. The time comes when certain individuals stand out from the crowd by virtue of their abilities. These people will be held and kept happy only by a share in the agency's ownership, with all the prestige (as well as the difficulties) that this involves. But note one thing. The agency owners must sense this need and meet it before the individual begins to show dissatisfaction. If the pressure comes from the employee, the ownership transfer is tainted. The relationship is hurt. "I had to put a gun to his head before I got it!" remarked one good man who recently acquired a piece of an agency. How long do you think he will remain in this shop?

Be sure you make the sharing in ownership a real one. It must include a sharing of the real responsibility and true authority. If you continue to exercise control, which you should in many cases, but also insist on retaining for yourself all real authority, your employee's share in the ownership becomes nothing but a worry with none of the pleasures that should reside in it, one of the greatest of which is a real say in formulating the agency's plans and destiny.

Each of the other parts of your total compensation package can exert a powerful effect on holding good people. They'll each be influenced to different degrees by the various elements that make up the total package, but a sound profit-sharing plan will probably be of most value after current salary and a share in the ownership of the agency.

Publicize Your Benefits

It's just human nature to take for granted something that keeps on coming in month after month and year after year. This is particularly true of your employee benefit programs which are designed to be there when people need them (as in the case of insurance programs) or which continue to build up values for the benefit of the employee at some distant retirement date.

So, tell your people what you're doing for them; tell them how much it's costing you; tell them what it'd cost them to go out and buy these programs on their own. Don't be bashful. You're paying out a pile of cash for these programs and you don't get any benefit from them unless your people know what you're doing for them and appreciate it.

How About Restrictive Agreements?

Many agencies ask their key people to sign agreements, in consideration of their employment, that they won't go into competition with the agency for a period of time after they leave its employ. The agreement probably also will provide that they can't work on the account of any agency client for the same period. It's not an easy matter to draft such a document that will stand up in court, but it can be done and I know agencies who have collected damages under such agreements.

While you probably should ask all your key people to sign noncompetition agreements as a matter of good business practice, don't count on them heavily to help hold your people. Because the agency business is so highly personal, no legal document can make an unhappy employee stay with you. And if he's unhappy, you probably wouldn't be happy with the work he's doing for you anyway.

Realistically, all such an agreement can be expected to do is to make it a little harder for departing employees to take some of your business with them and, possibly, get you some monetary compensation if they do. But against this you'll have to weigh the time you'll have to spend, the legal fees you'll incur, and the publicity you'll create if you decide to go to court. How much better it would be to work hard to make all your accounts *agency* accounts so no one employee could take them with him even if he tried. This seems to be the way to build a sound and long-lasting agency business.

15

The Contact Function

In any client-agency relationship the contact function is the hyphen; it is the interface that enables the two organizations to work together; it is the conduit through which information is transmitted from client to agency or from agency to client; in the eyes of the client the agency contact people are the agency; to the agency staff the contact people speak for the client.

In the agency scheme of things the contact function serves three main purposes — to see that the client's business is handled properly, professionally, and efficiently; to see that the agency retains, or better yet increases, the business; and to see that the agency handles the business at a profit.

So the contact function is a far cry from the impersonal mechanical transmittal of information the first paragraph might imply. Rather than being a mere messenger, the contact man must understand the thinking behind the ideas he's transmitting; he must be able to relate them to the client's whole program; he must be able to explain them clearly, completely, and convincingly. If he can't do this, chances are the ideas aren't right and he should try to get them changed.

Guidelines for Handling the Client's Account

It seems pretty obvious that if the contact people don't handle the client's business properly, there soon won't be any business to handle. So, it's important to sit down once in a while and ponder what it takes to handle an account properly.

Understanding

As one Texas advertiser put it in a seminar attended by agency people, "It is essential that the agency understand the client and its business; what it has to sell and how it sells it; the way the client thinks; its internal policies, problems, and bottlenecks; the pressures of time on top client advertising personnel." This is a primary responsibility of the agency's contact people.

Only by steady contact with everyone concerned with the client's promotional activities can the agency learn about all phases of the client's business. Don't forget that the client has been at this all his business life; yet we come in and are expected to advise him authoritatively on matters that may have troubled him for years.

All the information and rapport we can accumulate will be little enough to save us from bad breaks and make our advice worth listening to. Only personal contact can give us this real feel of a business. If we don't get it, we stay in the dark and our marketing recommendations are correspondingly limited or downright incorrect.

But we must go far beyond surface knowledge of a business and try to enter into the hopes, aspirations, and ideals of the people who run it. This sympathetic understanding of clients is of the utmost importance.

Never make the mistake of assuming that the only reason people are in business is to make money. This may be true in some cases, but the reason why most people bust themselves on a job, working at it nights and Sundays if necessary, far transcends the desire to get rich.

It may be ambition—such a person wants to be the biggest in his field. It may be for the sake of the children—he or she wants to leave them something better than he or she had. It may be to improve the world or its people. It may be to prove to detractors that he or she is a bigger and better person than they thought. It may be simply that he or she has become fascinated with the ramifications and possibilities in the field.

Remember that to get this understanding of the client, without which no advertising program can be truly successful, there is no substitute for frequent personal contact with every person and every area concerned with selling the client's goods. Rather than saying, "This is what I think," be able to say, "This is what I know; I was there."

Build a Partnership Relation

The contact group should strive to build a true partnership relation with the client where agency and client keep each other fully informed, where unpleasant surprises seldom arise because each is truthful and forthright with the other. This kind of attitude, which arises from steady contact, makes the agency a true partner in the client's success, with a priceless inside knowledge of the details of his or her business. A client is slow to fire an agency that has acquired this feel for his or her business, this personal friendship with suppliers or customers, this entreé into business areas and confabs from which the outsider is completely barred.

An agency that has achieved this partnership relation should not become complacent. Just as if it were employed by the client as sales manager, it should constantly be looking for trouble spots, trying to improve what may seem to be a satisfactory situation.

The more an agency has become an insider in the advertiser's business, the better chance it has to hold on to the account. Consider for a moment how an agency contact man may become so familiar with his accounts, on such terms of personal friendship with the advertiser's people, that he moves with the account from agency to agency. This is an example of the power of insidedness — and it is also a hint to keep both the contact man and the account happy, so as not to be confronted with this unhappy development.

Build a Comprehensive Plan

The agency, spearheaded by its contact people, and the client must work out a comprehensive advertising plan to achieve the client's goals. The plan should spell out the objectives to be reached and the ways of doing so. It should demonstrate creative thinking by the agency in conducting a successful search for the uncommon solution to a common problem.

The plan should provide for periodic review of results with the client to determine whether the advertising has been effective. The measure to be applied here is not whether the advertising has won a hatful of awards (however pleasant and flattering to the ego of the creative people that may be) nor even whether the client is enthusiastic about it. The true measure should be whether the advertising has achieved its real purpose — to sell what the client wants to sell.

Who Should Contact Whom?

Smart agencies, I think, are those that spread the contact chores around so that people in one organization get to know their counterparts in the other. The account executive is primarily responsible for client contact and will probably do the great bulk of it personally, but it never hurts once in a while to take along some of the troops who are doing the detailed work — a writer or artist or media man depending on need. Take the boss along once in a while, too.

On the client's side, contact by the agency should go further than just the top people in the client's organization. It's fine to have the boss pleased with us. But it's equally important to sell everyone else who has anything to say about the company's promotion work or who is affected by it.

Particularly important are the sales manager and his or her salespeople. They may not be consulted about the advertising. Frequently it is handed to them on a platter, which obviously should not be done. When this is the case, they often will blame the advertising for their own deficiencies or failures.

If the client hasn't had sense enough to mesh the advertising with his or her sales operation and make one feed into the other, the agency should do all in its power to remedy this weakness. The agency will receive valuable help from the sales division, and the sales people will be far better disposed toward the advertising if they have had something to do with it.

The only way to discover this situation and remedy it is by personal contact with all concerned with sales. That goes for the channels of distribution as well. Contact with the trade is a form of client contact that is often neglected; yet the avenues of distribution constitute a most important aspect of the entire promotion.

Note the effect it has on the big shot when we, the agency, come back to her with information we have accumulated out in the sticks, where even she has not been for a dog's age. "These people really know my business," she says. "That's a good agency."

Technical Follow-Through

The agency can't handle the client's advertising properly without competent follow-up throughout the shop. By this I mean the professional, workman-like performance of all the steps needed to implement the advertising plan — production, media buying, estimating, and billing, to name just a few. As the agency's chief point of contact with the client, the one who gets egg on the face when something goes wrong, the account executive must be responsible for seeing that the agency performs all of these implemental functions properly and on time.

The Contact Report

The contact report (or conference report or call report), that simple, obvious, essential detail of good agency practice, is not in proper use by one agency out of ten.

What is meant by "proper use"? Here are a few questions and answers that may be illuminating:

First, who writes contact reports? Every individual who is in contact with the client, in person, by mail, or by telephone. That means the boss, the account executive if there is one, and the agency treasurer or bookkeeper who may be discussing some billing procedure.

Second, when is it written? The same day as the conversation takes place or the instructions are received, if this is possible. People forget mighty fast.

Third, how do you make sure that all these different individuals produce contact reports? This task is difficult. Some individual in the agency must have, as part of his or her responsibility, the job of spotting the contacts and seeing that the decisions are recorded. Soon it will become apparent that some people pick up the good habit readily and can be relied upon to report. Others, however, usually the boss or some other person whose contacts are infrequent, will forget. They are best spotted by watching the correspondence and enlisting the help of the telephone operator. Retroactively, records are kept complete by checking every campaign started, every job undertaken, and every agency expenditure made for the client, and making sure that a contact report exists that contains the details and the proper authorization.

Fourth, who gets copies of contact reports? Everyone in the agency who is concerned with the activity recorded, and everyone in the client's organization who is similarly interested.

Fifth, what happens to these copies? They should be carefully filed, preferably in loose-leaf books under each client's name, with a file cross-indexed by decisions.

Sixth, do you need a contact report when the price or the decision has already been covered in some other written form, such as an order or a letter? Yes. Let there be one place where all these vital decisions are regularly recorded. Otherwise they will be scattered so widely that you never can find them when you need them most.

With properly kept records, even years later it should be possible to reconstruct every campaign, every step in every agency job, together with who authorized what and, if possible, why.

The factors that make it so difficult to maintain complete records of all contacts and decisions are, of course, pressure of other jobs, procrastination, the feeling that memoranda and letters are all that are needed, and plain laziness.

Among the benefits of well-kept contact reports are preventing postmortem arguments with the client, the coordination of all concerned in both the client's and the agency's organizations, and the instant availability of relevant facts in emergencies, or when some individual is sick or on vacation and someone else has to pinch-hit.

There are some less obvious benefits, too. Contact reports circulated among all those in the agency interested in this particular client may well result in constructive suggestions often from the least-expected sources. That is if such suggestions are invited, as of course they should be. Nobody has a monopoly on brains.

Also, in the give and take of the agency-client relationship, too many decisions are made off the top of the head by all parties. Contact reports confirming the course of action contemplated give us the chance for a second look, and avoid the misunderstandings that so often wreck an otherwise delightful relationship.

So the contact report is not simply something that is good to have if you can take time for it. It is the agency's most reliable protection against forgetfulness, change of personnel, or undeserved blame for someone else's wrong decisions. With the large sums of money involved in today's advertising operations, with the dangers to the agency's survival that may result from misunderstandings, the contact report is of fundamental importance.

Contact's Role in Holding Clients

Frequent client contact by agency people of standing and authority is a vital essential for holding and expanding business.

As any rancher can tell you, keeping your fences mended is the best way to prevent cattle escaping. Business jumps from one agency to another for one or more of three main reasons: actual client dissatisfaction, justified or not; promises of more for their money from competing agencies; and some form of conflict or other difficulty originating in the agency.

The first two are the ones the agency needs to know about in time to take measures to improve the situation. The ability to smell smoke is a great agency asset. Big changes spring from the small beginnings of a little discontent, perhaps with our charges or the way our secretary talks over the phone. Sitting in the client's lap, as a California friend expresses it, is a vantage point from which to recognize and correct immediately any little vexation that may soon assume alarming proportions. Only contact, frequent, never perfunctory, and with the right people in the client's organization, makes rapport possible.

It isn't enough to sell our clients. We have to keep them sold. If we don't, someone else will.

Don't forget that a client with whom we sit down today may have just met with a competitor of ours, not because he contemplates a change, you understand, but because it is his duty to his company to learn as much as possible about other available agency services.

Frequent personal contacts not only spread the mortar of friendship between the stones of your relationship, they enable the agency to be selling itself constantly, which it must do, considering how many other agencies are waving special inducements under the client's nose.

It's tempting to say that agencies hold business by rendering good service; yet, while the production of effective advertising for clients is an essential for holding business, it is by no means the only one. Sadly enough, we all know of cases in which agencies have lost accounts on which they have done excellent jobs. This was because of changes in the advertiser's organization, unexpected developments within the advertiser's own field not anticipated by the agency, and policy shifts, desirable or otherwise. Competitive solicitations by other agencies also cause many account changes, especially where better deals are offered, financially or with longer credit terms.

Definitely, to have the best possible chance to hang onto desirable business, the agency must add constant attention to the client to its good service program.

Finally, we need to remember that agency service, and indeed advertising itself, is constantly on trial in the mind of the man who pays the bills. It calls forth an entirely different attitude from that enjoyed by other expenditures for more concrete or more easily evaluated commodities or services. This state of mind is something to be combatted constantly, not only by superlative service but also by physical contact on a regular basis, scheduled in advance and augmented by special calls whenever required.

The more frequently the agency sits down and thrashes out problems that confront the advertiser, not only those of advertising, but also those of all marketing, of which advertising is a part, the more uncertainty fades and certainty and reassurance grow.

Handling an Account at a Profit

Right off the bat I want to remind all you good readers that advertising agencies are in business to make a profit and should not be bashful about it. Clients don't object to their agencies' making a reasonable profit; in fact they expect them to be good enough businessmen so they will earn a profit. If you come across a client that doesn't feel this way, watch out!

As the person most involved in all phases of the agency-client relationship, the contact man is the one properly charged with so handling his account that the agency comes out with a profit. How does he do it? He has to adopt the right attitudes and back these up by actions consistent with these attitudes.

Be Money-Minded

From the very beginning of the relationship let the client know that you are concerned with money matters. Start right out by discussing fully and frankly what you bill for and how. Be specific.

The fatal procedure is to start on an account with a vague and generalized understanding on both sides of how the agency will be compensated and then try to fix things up later when the agency wakes up to the fact that it is losing money on the operation. This is, of course, due to the human reluctance to face facts or to talk money during the delicate days of the honeymoon. Don't fall into this trap!

When talking about a specific job, go beyond what has to be done to do it right and mentally figure what it's going to cost the agency to do it. Maybe there's an equally effective way that will cost the agency less.

Try to inculcate this money-mindedness into all your associates in the agency. It's only human nature for a dedicated creative person to want to keep on redoing an advertisement in search of perfection. Aside from the fact that there is no such thing as true perfection, you should indoctrinate your people with the economic facts of life and in particular the law of diminishing returns. In advertising, as in any other creative pursuit, there must come a time to say with Macbeth, "Hold! Enough!"

Be Businesslike
By this possibly enigmatic statement, I mean never undertake a job unless both agency and client clearly understand what is to be done, who is to do it, and what the costs are to be. In other words there should be an initial estimate. This should provide for adjustments in case the ground rules are changed part way through the job. It should be clearly understood, for example, that once an advertisement has been approved by the client, any changes to be made in it will be charged for in addition to the original estimate.

Another way to manifest a businesslike attitude is to avoid making off-the-cuff promises that you may or may not be able to keep. When a client asks if final production on an ad can be completed by Friday, don't just say, "sure." How much better to say something like, "I'm sure we can, but I can't promise until I talk to my production people."

Then you can call the client the next day and say, "Yes, we can meet that deadline with no strain," or, maybe, "We can do it, but it'll take several hundred dollars worth of overtime by the typographers. OK?"

This situation brings us to the last businesslike action I'm going to discuss. This is to be sure, whenever there's a change in an estimate for a job, particularly an increase in cost, to get written confirmation. Maybe a simple conference report will suffice, but be sure to have something. It may be some time before the job gets billed and human memory can be short. Why take a chance on arguments and ruffled feelings when a simple businesslike procedure can avoid it?

Some Emotional and Psychological Considerations

Of individuals it is often said, "We get back from the world just about what we give it." This is another way of saying that each person's attitude toward life strongly influences his success or failure. Without a doubt, the agency's attitude toward its clients is as influential in holding or losing business as its creative ability. Attitude is expressed in the manner, the matter, and the frequency of contacts.

There is a strong emotional element in the agency-client relation of which sensitive advertising people are acutely aware. It is almost like a marriage.

Yet you always have against you the fact that no matter how you phrase it, you are an outsider looking in. You are not a part of the client's organization, on its payroll, rising or falling with its successes or failures. You have other business on your books. If the client fails, you will survive.

These are the emotional background feelings of which you must be aware. As much as possible, you must eliminate them and substitute for them the feelings characteristic of the ideal employer-employee relationship. Literally, you must become, to the greatest possible extent, a member of the client's company.

I'm not suggesting expediency or even a shadow of deceit. You can do your best job only if you feel this way about your client. If again you nod and say, "Why, of course," I ask you honestly to compare your feelings about your clients with those suggested as essential. Are you working with these people, or just for them?

The reason so many advertising accounts follow one individual from agency to agency is not, as so often believed, that person's familiarity with the client's business. It is almost invariably the fact that the man in question has established with the client this personal trust, this emotional relationship. As the client so often puts it, "He talks our language," or "He's really a member of the family, not just a business associate." This is definitely emotional, and you never want to underestimate the power of emotion in our business.

There's an important corollary to this. If individuals in the agency establish an emotional relationship with the client, thereby becoming influential in holding the business, the agency should establish the same sort of relationship with these individuals so it will be sure to hold onto their services.

When I talk about establishing an emotional relationship with the client, I'm talking about developing a true personal understanding. This is an understanding by the agency person of the basic forces behind the advertiser's activities. What really makes him or her tick?

Why is he or she spending this money for advertising? Is it only to facilitate and increase sales? Or are other ambitions and aims involved? Frequently the client is entirely unconscious of these hidden urges. But the more the agency person understands them, the more helpful he or she can be, and the more likely to continue the relationship.

Such an understanding by an account executive expresses itself in a sympathy and warmth of which the client is instantly aware. If he or she put these feelings into words, they would be, "This is more than a business relationship. He wants my account, and he wants to work with me, not only because of the money he will make in the process, but also because he is interested in what I am trying to accomplish."

I hasten to say that I'm not advising you to simulate this sympathy. In the first place, this is something you are unlikely to be able to fake. In the second place, insincerity once detected is strong poison. No, this attitude, this desire to team up with the hidden motives of others, provided they are worthy ones, is one of the strongest of all feelings that holds human beings together only when it is genuine. It goes not only for agency-client relationships, but for all business and personal contacts in life.

Remember, too, that while honest advice is essential, so is horse sense. There are bound to be times when advice is resented and angrily resisted. The client has a psychological problem of his or her own, often one inherent in power. A person in position of authority, especially on the spending of large sums of money, may well be sensitive about his or her prerogatives. One does not gratuitously step on this person's toes.

Never say to a client, no matter what the provocation, "Well, we have a few other jobs to do, you know." All very true but, to the client, his or her account is the only one in your shop. If you don't make him or her feel that you are operating as if this were the case, watch out for trouble.

16

The Creative Function

The creative function covers a lot of territory. It embraces the complete expression of the promotional plan in words, pictures, or anything else that can convey the message.

One major component of the whole creative package is art in all its forms — rough layout, comprehensive, finished art, photography.

Another is copy, from the few simple words needed to convey the message to a motorist passing a billboard at 65 m.p.h. to a full page of solid copy explaining a complicated proposition. Don't forget, either, the completely different problems in combining selling and some entertainment in a television commercial that may last only 30 seconds or less.

Television also requires a liberal dash of the theatrical, including the proper selection of actors, decisions as to lighting, music, and the like. Most of these activities are left to the studio actually producing the film or tape, but the agency must be capable of supervising them so it can be sure the final product is right. This broadcast production responsibility is usually included in the agency's overall creative function. In addition, this department is usually charged with supervising the business aspects of television such as assuring that the right prints or tapes are sent to the right stations and that proper payments are made to the talent.

Point-of-purchase materials make up another important part of the whole promotional package. Sometimes a separate department is set up to handle everything connected with these materials, but more frequently they are assigned to the regular agency departments including, of course, the creative.

Occasionally an agency will become involved in such activities as the design of a new package or even a logotype for a client. It then becomes part of a highly specialized design function and usually charges a special fee for this service.

Now that I've outlined the extent of the area covered by the creative function, let's get down to some specifics.

How Do You Write Good Copy?

First off, I can't really tell you how to write good copy or make a good layout or produce a good television commercial. You have to be born with a gift for this kind of thing just as a musician must be in order to play the piano well. In all these arts you can learn to perform adequately by hard work and training, but the finished product isn't art unless you are an artist.

All I can do here is give you some ideas as to what you should do before putting pen to paper to give yourself the best possible chance. After that you're on your own. Since these same general principles apply to art and broadcast production I'm really going to be talking about all of them, although I'll employ copy terms in doing so. When I say "copy" or "write" just mentally substitute "art" and "draw" or "commercial" and "produce," according to your main interest.

Build on a Sound Foundation

Actually, the basic thinking, the selling strategy evolved from knowledge of the product or service, its present channels of distribution, and its impact upon the ultimate consumer are all more important than how you interpret them. A sound basic selling idea with only fair copy will sell better than one based on a fallacious premise even though it may be interpreted and presented with the utmost brilliance.

Soundness should be the aim of all creative thinking. This statement may seem obvious, but actually a great deal of advertising concerns itself with being different, with new and unusual approaches, with devices aimed at attracting attention. An essential first step that must precede any copy production or even planning is the most painstaking analysis of the product or service to be sold.

First, listen to your clients carefully and with discrimination. Usually advertisers know what they are talking about when they detail the virtues of their products and their marketing situation. Sometimes, however, they are surprisingly inaccurate in both these appraisals. So, the first thing you must do is to interpret wisely and check the accuracy of the client's ideas. Take and use whatever is evidently realistic, but substitute truth and exactness for errors and inaccuracies.

Next, listen to the trade. By trade I mean not only all channels of distribution, but all communications media such as trade and consumer publications that provide an astonishing amount of information about any product or service whose success or failure has such a strong effect upon their own pocketbooks.

Finally, listen to the consumer. Talk to people who use your client's product and to those who don't. In each case, find out why. Quite possibly, the search for a product story may indicate the need for a change in the product itself, its price, or its manner of distribution. No use telling your story well unless it's a good one. What consumers want to know is, "What's in it for me?" This oft-repeated statement needs to be pasted in every advertising man's hat. No basic slant is worth a whoop unless it answers that question.

If the product is selling well against competition, there are definite reasons for its success. These are the facts that belong in its advertising — all of them. The best advertising tells the product's story as well as, or better than, the product tells it. What people want from advertising is information and often they get too darned little of it.

If you look straight at copy creativity, you will not even begin to write until you are convinced that good copy will sell the product. If you are in any doubt about that because of the product's own character, stop, look, and listen. No amount of advertising, no matter how good, will sell a poor product. You may, and probably will, get initial sales. Without repeats, however, these cannot build a business.

The ideal advertising to offer your client is based on a foundation of research and ascertained marketing facts. Once you have constructed this foundation, it is permissible, and indeed desirable, to implement your knowledge with brilliance, provided always that this does not depart from selling fundamentals.

Good ideas are sound, simple, easily remembered, true and honest, and attuned to the consumer's predilections. If they are also unusual, striking, and ingenious, well and good. These three, however, are secondary requirements compared with the basic six.

Develop the Proper Attitude

In the development of an advertising program both client and agency are shooting for something unusual, something sure-fire, and something new, a reliable stimulus that will interest an audience and make it take action. To this endeavor the agency's creative staff brings its skills as expert consultants, specialists in advertising communications. The client brings a desire for increased sales and profits and also an abiding interest in the qualities of its product or service.

This combination of factors can, at times, result in some pretty substantial emotional involvements. So it's important that from the very beginning the agency's creative people adopt the proper attitude to the client, the product, and the consumer. Toward the client they should adopt the attitude of complete frankness and honesty. They must always be true, if you will, to their own intellectual integrity and steadfastly avoid creating advertising designed purely to please the client.

The agency must chart the course of the advertising program, put on the brakes fast if anything seems likely to get out of control, and insist on solid foundations before building superstructures. It must resolve firmly to advise the client for his or her best interest.

Regarding the client's product or service, you, as a writer, must know your subject. By this I mean not only understand it in every aspect, but feel it, be in sympathy with it, and be possessed with a burning desire to extol its virtues. If what you're writing about doesn't seem to be of surpassing importance to you, you won't write anything important about it. Writers can write fluently about almost anything. They write convincingly, however (and this is advertising), only about something they believe. They can't fool themselves or their readers. What's more, if they are honest, they will admit it.

Regarding the potential user you are seeking to convince, your attitude must be one of interest and sympathy. What is he like? What is his background? What are his capacities? His weaknesses? His prejudices? His knowledge? How intelligent is he? And finally, to what favorable or unfavorable influences has he already been subjected in the area you are pursuing? Is it, so far as your case is concerned, virgin territory? Or is he already preconditioned for or against you?

You must be willing to put yourself in the shoes of the consumer. Like an orator or actor, you can sway your audience only if you identify yourself with it—in short, become your audience at the moment of creativity.

Use the Line of Least Resistance

For every product or service there is one best way to sell it. This is the line of least resistance to the selected user's mind, supposedly discovered by analyzing what that product does for that consumer. Somewhere there is a common ground on which the product you are selling and the people to whom you sell it meet. When you find that, a good part of your work is done. The rest is craftsmanship.

In essence, great copy involves a preconceived correct selling slant and expresses it in the one absolutely best manner to get into the reader's head (and his heart) with the maximum impact and staying power. This means that, even if you are a great writer, you must know your subject. The most polished, terse, compact, beautifully expressed collection of words is just so much applesauce unless it says something. Too often magnificent writing is this and this alone.

There is one best way to say what you have to say. You may hit it first crack out of the box, especially if you have written at white heat. Such a performance may need only some polishing, some refinement. It was right to begin with and the less you fuss with it, the better.

Most of us, however, write many versions before the best one takes shape. Once you've done the job as well as you can, set it aside for a while if you have the time. Then review it and either decide that it's right on the nose or scrap it and start over. Remember, too, there are few pieces of writing, no matter how good, that cannot be improved by condensation. There are many ways, long and short, to express a thought. Can you say it better in fewer words? Fine! But don't cut merely for the sake of cutting.

Beware the trap of seeking attention for its own sake. The commonsense way to attack such problems as these is to ask yourself, when considering any procedure or selling strategy, one fundamental question: "What final mental result am I shooting for?" Not what *first* mental result, but what *final* mental result. Please note the important distinction. Not just attention, which any salesman can get by standing on his head in the prospect's office, but conviction and desired final action. If this question were asked on every projected selling or advertising campaign, we would save our clients large bundles of cash money.

This sort of thing is much harder to sell to clients. What they want is something different—attention getters. I know that; I've been sitting across from clients for quite a while. I know what they buy most easily. But that's not the answer, is it? So, you may say, how come you see so little great advertising? Once every couple of months, if you read advertising constantly, you encounter great copy. Not much oftener, I'm afraid. Well, how often do you encounter a great painting, an outstanding play, or a top piece of musical composition? Why should it surprise us that great advertising is just as rare? It is of comparable difficulty.

Managing the Creative Function

In the preceding section I talked about the need for a sound foundation on which to base a creative effort, the need to develop a proper attitude, and the importance of finding the one best way to tell the story. Once you've instilled in your people this basic philosophical approach to creating good advertising, how do you, as agency principal, go about trying to insure that your agency's output will have that spark of superior creativity that distinguishes the really successful agency from the merely adequate one?

Top Management's Responsibility
You should continually assess and evaluate your agency's performance in creativity. Is it doing merely an honest and workmanlike job of promotion complete with a sincere interest in the client's welfare, but with little creative spark? Or is there real creativity? What do I mean by that?

I think that greatness in all of the communications arts—literature, music, sculpture, painting, and advertising—has one single characteristic. It is the injection of life into matter previously dead or dormant. Without this, the communication soon dies; with it, it lives. So, continually review the agency's ouput and ask yourself, "Is it alive?" Even if you can't write great copy yourself, you can recognize it when you see it, give valuable help to the creator, keep the feet on the ground while the head is in the clouds. Manage all you want to see that the sales message and all the other musts are included, but don't monkey with the words if they sing.

Keep the Client's Hands Off

Once a piece of great copy has been written it must be steered past the client with its inspiration intact, which brings us to the whole subject of client involvement with creativity. He pays the bills and sees no reason why he should not contribute his best judgment to the finished creative product. "You know advertising," he says, "and we know our particular business. If we both contribute what we know best, the final product should be as effective as possible."

This may sound fine but, far more often than not, it just won't work. Take a lesson from lawyers and doctors. When you hire one of those to keep you out of jail or the hospital, you don't tell them how to do it. You put the responsibility where it belongs, on the guy who is supposed to know the answers.

To an almost equal degree, the responsibility for top creative thinking should rest with the agency. The client's function is to be sure the ideas suggested are realistic, that they do not conflict with facts which the client knows more about than the agency. Advertisers should not set themselves up as authorities on copy, art, media selection, or any other functions that are part of agency creative work.

As early as possible in the relationship with your clients you should clearly establish that the agency is the expert advertising practitioner. Properly and tactfully approached, clients are glad to find agencies that want to take on the entire responsibility for how and where and when the advertiser's money is spent. They have much more respect for the agency that knows its business and does not hesitate to say so. Agencies have failed to land accounts for many and varied reasons, but I have yet to hear of a solicitation that failed because the agency had the courage of its convictions. You don't have to be cocky about it. You have to recognize that there are definite factual areas in which the advertiser must be consulted. Say this at the outset, so you won't seem to be assuming knowledge you do not possess. But when it comes to creation, this is where you know the answers, and the less your suggestions are interfered with the better the results will be.

So, have the courage of your convictions. If you feel that the creative work is exactly right—not just fairly good or calculated to please—submit it to the client and be prepared to fight for it. By all means avoid the all-too-common error of showing the client several different versions for his choice. Set the agency up as the creative expert, and stick to your guns!

How About Quality Control?

As the advertising agency grows in size and the principals can no longer be involved personally in all the planning and execution of creative activities, it becomes necessary to develop some central supervisory body of executives who will periodically review the agency's operations and make recommendations concerning them. It is best to keep this group as small as possible; the more people you have on it the more difficult it is to get them together, and the more chance conflicting opinions will arise.

This body is usually called a *plans board* and consists of the agency principals and the top creative thinkers. To serve on such a board is an honor and a recognition of the fact that the individual is an important factor in the agency's success.

It is desirable to decide in advance just how wide a scope the plans board should encompass. In some agencies this committee reviews copy, supervising the creative output only. In others, especially the larger shops, the plans board may well watch all the agency activities: contact, research, internal functioning, new business activities, and so on.

Usually the plans board functions as an advisory body only. It makes recommendations to individuals or departments within the agency. To operate properly the board must meet at some preset time very week or, at least, every other week.

The operation of a plans board is based on the principle that creative work, the agency's only exclusive asset, is too important and valuable a commodity to be entrusted to any one individual, no matter how able. The plans board acts as a safeguard, and in the overall work of the agency, the final decisions are those of the committee, which represents the agency. Once this fundamental principle is understood and accepted by all concerned, the way is clear to an agency operation which insures that the client receives the best possible service.

Principles of Pretesting

With advertising being such an intangible influence and one almost impossible to measure in most cases I can't imagine why any good advertising person would fail to test the creative product in advance whenever possible.

If facts are available, fine, but in the many instances where uncertainty prevails, you're better off to pretest. This is commonly called copy testing although it usually goes beyond this to include all types of advance experimentation with appeals and methods of promotion.

Probably a lot more copy testing would be done were it not for the misunderstanding these words create. Too often we think tests will give us facts, when these actually are not obtainable. We expect testing to do the impossible, instead of being thankful for any indications it may give us of the right road.

Principle No. 1, then, must necessarily be: Don't expect the impossible.

Principle No. 2 is try to test only one thing at a time. It is surprising how often this rule is broken. Where more than one factor is at work (such as headline and body copy, or headline and picture), it is impossible to segregate one from the other, and determine which is doing the job. Thus, when testing the comparative effectiveness of two advertisements, in split runs, let us say, let them be exactly alike in all respects except one—the heading or the body copy or the picture.

This maintenance of uniformity in all but one respect also holds for time of insertion and size of space. Don't compare advertisements run in July and January, when seasonal factors may be operating. (And they are often powerful in ways you easily may overlook.k.) By the same token, never try to compare advertisements of differing sizes. It won't work to cut results in two from one advertisement twice the size of another.

Principle No. 3 of copy testing is a warning: Beware of laboratory tests. These fool many of us. They are easy, tempting, and usually deceptive. Laboratory tests include all opinion tests with such questions as, "Which of these advertisements do you like best?" The question may be asked of an office associate or a nationwide consumer jury. The laboratory method is somewhat more reliable when we use coupons and costs per inquiry to indicate the comparative power of various advertisements. But this still indicates that we are foggy in our thinking as to what we are trying to find out. If you want to know how many people will send for a free cookbook, that's one thing. But it proves nothing about how many people will respond to this particular selling slant and buy your product off the shelves.

Principle No. 4 is it is often practicable and economically desirable to test small at first. Especially as we adhere to our rule of testing only one factor at a time, we need to seek small space rather than large for our comparisons. We have to be careful, however, that our small space insertions do not become invalid when we eventually use larger space. This, of course, is a matter of judgment and horse sense.

How about pretesting television commercials? Will these principles permit realistic testing of this important form of advertising?

It is extremely doubtful. Elaborate theater showings of commercials are often conducted before audiences to find out what is liked and what is disliked. Some general indications may be the result. Again, however, how close are the conditions of this test to the actual conditions under which the commercial would be viewed at home? What will buying reactions be in the supermarket? Will consumers behave in stores as they do in your theater? Alas! One fears that many other factors are present in real life that cannot be duplicated in laboratory tests.

═17═
The Implemental Functions

Since this book is concerned primarily with agency management, it can't go into detail on those many highly specialized functions that insure that the advertising message, once created, actually appears. Some of these occur before, some during, and others after the creative process. Without them, the advertisement can't possibly appear at the right time, in the right place, and in the right physical form.

The agency principal can't be an expert in all these fields, but he or she should be familiar with the basic functions in order to evaluate the job of those entrusted with the day-to-day operations of the departments involved.

Here is a brief description of what I've called implemental functions, with some of the basic areas each should cover.

Marketing

The term marketing is often used in a broad sense covering business activities far beyond those that normally belong under this term. Just what is marketing? Marketing is moving a product or service from conception to consumption, with growth and profit. The word "moving" is the key to this definition. Any activity that contributes to that movement is marketing. Anything else may be called planning, research and development, budgeting, or something else. The movement to which I refer takes place through definite channels of distribution, with the help of skilled individuals in various parts of the distribution chain.

A good agency should be intensely interested in marketing. It should know exactly what its client is doing to facilitate this movement. It should be able to spot what is weak and emphasize what is strong. If only for its own self-protection, since its advertising is designed to help sales, it must be sure nothing interferes with the implementation of its plans and promotional material. The agency has to help keep the channels clear and the merchandise flowing. Motion is of the essence.

Advertising's Place in the Marketing Mix

There are, of course, three main causations of any sale. They are, in order of importance, desirability, availability, and awareness. Too few agencies realize that the first two of these essentials must be assured, and not just assumed, before spending advertising money.

The product (or service) must first of all be desirable, that is, needed and adapted to local conditions, habits, and prejudices better than competing products (or services), as well as competitively priced.

Second, it must be easily obtainable. It must be available without going from store to store or outlet to outlet to procure it. Further it must be available to the extent that it has the backing and approval of the retailer and/or wholesaler, so it will be given preferential handling by all those who move it along to possible buyers. Not only must it be in the outlets frequented by consumers, it must be brought forcibly to their favorable notice.

The third element in the correct marketing formula is awareness, which is what we are supposed to build in the minds of prospective users mostly by one or another form of advertising.

It is often a shock to discover that we may obtain greater awareness for less money by local store favor and display than by national advertising. A good store display and a bit of a push from the man behind the counter often will sell even a non-advertised product. On the other hand, the best advertising in the world cannot sell a product if its user has difficulty in obtaining it.

The Agency's Responsibility

The agency owes it to itself and its client to do all it can to ensure that its plans and creative work are not stepping up to the plate with two strikes on them. This may call for a lot of homework and even some fieldwork before you put pencil to paper. Is the product or service right? Have you satisfied yourself that the product or service you're being asked to advertise fills a need or desire of the user? Is it attractive? Is it priced right?

If the product is normally sold through stores, it's not too difficult or expensive to run a practical test. Set up a sort of retail laboratory using maybe a half-dozen outlets strategically located in various parts of the country, plus a special cash inducement to compensate the store owners for having their shops used as a proving ground.

Now, with the approval of the advertiser, you can work towards evolving a selling formula originating at the point of sale in which the three basic marketing elements operate in proper sequence. You may need point-of-sale material, demonstrators, or other measures. This process will let you discover under real-life conditions whether the product is desirable and what happens when it is available under favorable circumstances.

The least that can happen after such an experiment is an improved picture of the product's character, and trade attitudes and consumer reactions to it.

Don't carry the measurement of desirability to the extreme of passing moral judgment, however, refusing to advertise a product just because it may be designed with planned obsolescence, or because you may think the client would be better off in the long run adopting a policy of fewer sales and more permanent user satisfaction rather than keeping the products moving off the shelves. Clients tend to be a bit sensitive on such subjects. Perhaps some doubts may have occurred to them on catering to wasteful- ness, or making money out of user inertia. But they do not take kindly to having their conscience prodded on such ticklish matters. Better stick to your knitting and do the best you can with the job given you, always provided that the product is not harmful or dishonest, and does no harm to the consumer more serious than causing an unnecessary drain on his or her pocketbook.

How about availability? There's no better way to create ill will than to have a potential customer come into a store all set to try out a new product that he or she has seen advertised only to be told, "We don't have it in yet. Come back next week." The moral, of course, is don't let your client advertise until the product is available in the area where it's being advertised. The old belief that advertising creates distribution is a fallacy; it's putting the cart before the horse.

The best advice, probably, is to make haste slowly. Consolidate your position before advancing.

Let's consider how you might advise a client who's built up a successful local or regional operation and is thinking about going national. When he or she comes to you for advice, you might start out by saying, "Yes, it's been done. Let's see if it seems wise in your case." With this approach you avoid antagonizing the client.

An always relevant and constructive question is, "How much will this move cost you?" The answer to this requires an analysis by the client of his present relationship between sales and promotional expenditure. How many additional people will be reached by the national effort? Are they the kind of people who can and will buy the product?

Most important of all, granted the product is one that would meet a national demand, will it be on sale in the retail outlets at the time your advertising breaks? If it isn't, not only are you pouring money down a rat hole, you are antagonizing a lot of potential consumers who can't find your product and whose retailer may never even have heard of it.

If, by soothing and tactful treatment, the client has been convinced he or she should look realistically at the question of going national, the agency's next statement is this: "You have wisely developed your local situations profitably. Have you reached the saturation point, or are your present markets susceptible to further development with a promotional expenditure that shows you a profit?"

Usually, there is far more juice left in the orange you are squeezing than either you or the client realizes. It may be less glamorous than the new oranges hanging on the trees, but it is profitable juice, safe, and sure.

Suppose more intensive development is somewhat more expensive than the first results? How much more expensive? And how does it compare with the new expenses a national effort would incur? Yes, by all means, play it local first, thus gaining invaluable experience.

Go national only when local territories have been adequately exploited, and be sure you leave enough promotion money in them to retain the success you have won.

Go national only after wide enough distribution has been obtained to insure against customer disappointment.

Go national only when accurate figures show that this way you can now sell for less money than (or equal money to) the local market in terms of the relationship of total promotional expense to sales.

How do you learn these things? There are lots of sources. Start with data on distribution your client's sales department has gathered. Then check surveys available from the media. Many of them regularly make store checks in their own areas and will be glad to give you the information. Some of them will make special spot checks for you.

Then there's always specially commissioned research. You'll most likely want to retain an outside research organization for studies in motivation — what customers think of a product, what makes it desirable — and market research to check on distribution and dealer attitudes.

Who pays for this? There's more on this subject in the research section later in this chapter, but the basic rule should be this: If the research is for the education of the agency to help it produce better advertising, no charge to the client; if it's for the client's benefit to improve his product or its distribution, the client should pay.

Now Comes the Advertising
So, now that you've checked on desirability and availability you're ready to start planning, producing, and placing your advertising. This will call into play all the different functions and activities discussed throughout this book.

Media

The most brilliantly conceived and written advertisement isn't going to do anybody any good until the intended audience is exposed to it. This can be done in a great number of ways, from network television to skywriting. The media function selects the proper vehicle or combination of vehicles to present your advertising most effectively. When properly handled this can be a truly creative function.

Before going on to describe the media function let's take a moment to consider the recent widespread publicity about advertisers setting up their own in-house media functions. How common is this and what effect will it have on agency operations?

In answer to this question I would like to point out several important facts. First, client in-house media buying has been around for at least ten years and the agencies involved with those clients have been able to make the necessary adjustments to levels of income and the services that must be performed.

Second, the AAAA has estimated that only about two percent of media buying is now being done in-house.

Third, even when media buying moves in-house, the planning and some large parts of the actual buying (for example, spot TV buying) stays with the agency.

Fourth, when an agency loses the income from the billing taken over by the client, it is able to reduce costs by eliminating the employees who formerly handled the same functions at the agency. As a matter of fact, in one recent instance the client accomplished the takeover by simply transferring to its own payroll the media employees of the agency who had previously been doing the same work on the agency's payroll.

Another fact is that this movement has been confined to very large advertisers who spend upwards of $50 million and hence will have almost no effect on the great majority of agencies, particularly those of a size with which this book is mainly concerned. This $50 million figure was mentioned by a large advertiser at a recent meeting of the Association of National Advertisers as the smallest that could justify in-house media buying.

A final fact is that the growing use of fees as a means of compensating agencies makes it almost inevitable that any move to bring media buying in-house would result in discussions between client and agency over making equitable adjustments in agency compensation. After all, most advertisers expect all their suppliers, including their agencies, to make a profit on the work they do for them. If you have a client that doesn't think this way you're probably better off without him anyway.

To summarize my thoughts on client media buying in-house, I believe it will continue to exist and probably continue to grow, but will be confined to very large clients and should not materially affect agencies of a size to whom this book will primarily appeal. In any event, you'll need a media department for planning and to serve all of your clients who don't go in-house for media buying.

So, having had my say on this question, let's look at the major considerations in media selection.

What to Look for in Selecting Media

The basic rule for media selection can be stated: Buy where you will reach the most people of the type you want, when and where they are mostly likely to buy, with the most careful and efficient utilization of the client's money. This obviously goes way beyond the old criterion of how much it costs to get a thousand readers or viewers or hearers who are located where you want them. Here are a few of the other things to look at.

The influence of the medium.   Do those who see it or hear it respect it? Do they get from it important information in addition to its entertainment value? Is it essential to them or can they take it or leave it?

The appropriateness of the medium.   You are looking not only for numbers of people located where they can buy your product; you seek the type of people who will buy. Are these the kind of people who are reached by this medium?

The size of the medium.   Yes, costs per thousand usually go down as circulation increases, but at the same time the number of claims for the reader's attention go up. Might you do better to tell your story in a drawing room instead of Grand Central Station?

The success of the medium.   Is it on the way up or going down? This indicates the need for up-to-date information. Try to buy what a medium is today, not what it was last year.

Duplication.   Does the medium do the same job, practically, as others you are buying? Often this reinforcement is desirable, but it can be expensive.

These are only a few of the additional facts to consider. Add to them information about how long the life of the medium is, how many people see each copy, whether it's bought or free, guarantees of its circulation, any special racial or religious influence it may have, and you arrive at a pretty good picture of what you are really buying.

Astute and scholarly media analysis makes the advertising dollar go far. Also, as it should, it makes a most favorable impression on the client. Here is one of several ways in which the agency can justly claim superior knowledge and prove it. There is just as much call for creative thinking in the media department as in the realm of copy and plans.

Extra Values You Can Get from Media

Any publication can give you a very detailed breakdown of the kind of people it reaches—the demographics and maybe even psychographics of its audience—and where they live. Some even go so far as to break down their data by postal zip codes. But you can get help from media and their representatives in a lot of other ways too.

They'll be glad to give you geographical or even climatological differences in their areas that may affect your product's sales; they'll come up with data on the advertising activities of your client's competitors; they'll make store checks and market position studies; they have available all major research studies which they'll be glad to share with you. Try them out. You may be surprised how much help you can get.

How About Local Rates and Co-op Advertising?

Most newspapers, many radio stations, and some TV stations have local rates that are substantially lower than their national rates. The local rates are frequently not commissionable but almost always are so much lower that an agency for a client that qualifies to use local rates can add on its 17.65 percent markup and still save the client money. All non-commissionable local rate advertising placed through the agency is handled this way unless the agency is working under an overall fee arrangement calling for billing all outside purchases at net cost.

Let's look first at the handling of co-op advertising as it affects the agency for the manufacturer. You start with a definite understanding, in contract form, between the manufacturer and his outlets as regards advertising. This stipulates the amount each will pay towards the final amount expended for local advertising. Often the manufacturer will pay 50 percent of the cost of locally placed advertising, but it can run up to 75 percent or, in some cases, even 100 percent. The agency must be involved in the negotiations drawing up this agreement.

Generally the manufacturer and his agency determine the advertising approach and wording. It is not usually feasible to let local outlets change the material, since for cumulative effect all the advertising should tell the same story in the same way. Usually, therefore, this co-op advertising goes out in the form of mats for newspapers and tapes or films for broadcast media. The dealer's name is then added locally.

The dealer or other local outlet places the advertising at the local rate and pays for it in the normal course of business. Each month, then, the dealer sends tear sheets or affidavits of performance with copies of the bills to the manufacturer's agency. This agency reimburses the dealer in the agreed-upon ratio and, in turn, bills its manufacturer client for his or her share. The agency, of course, adds on the standard markup.

More and more large local outlets, such as department stores and distributors, are now employing their own agencies; this can complicate the co-op picture. When such a store participates in a co-op program it naturally has its agency place the advertising and also handle the production details needed to get the store's name added to the material from the manufacturer's agency, or even to produce the whole advertisement locally.

The local agency bills its client for its services including standard markup or commission and attaches all the necessary supporting papers. The store pays its agency and passes on to the manufacturer's agency its claim for reimbursement in accordance with the co-op contract. This is where it gets sticky because, certainly, the manufacturer's agency is entitled to compensation for creating the advertising that was used locally and yet one commission has already been paid to the local agency on the space or time.

There are probably as many ways to approach this problem as there are cooperative advertising plans. One, surely, might be for the client to share with his agency the savings the client realizes as a result of using local rates. Another would be for the agency to be paid a straight fee for creating the co-op advertising, without relating this directly to the space or time used to carry the message.

My purpose here is not to draw up a catalog of methods for paying the agency, but simply to point out the problem. Agency principals becoming involved in a co-op program should take good care to investigate fully this aspect of the agreement to insure that they will be properly compensated for their efforts.

Barter

Many years ago it was common for advertisers, like hotels, to pay for space or time by giving due bills that could be exchanged for room accommodations. In radio and TV the practice traditionally was involved with payment for distress time—and there's nothing so worthless as time that has gone by unsold.

Now a lead article in *Advertising Age* points out that the practice is spreading to cover payment for time bought in the regular manner on the basis of gross rating points or other standard criteria. The difference is that the time is paid for by merchandise—even including automobiles—or a combination of merchandise and cash. This can get pretty technical and most barter deals are arranged through specialized agencies in New York or Chicago.

You may never come face to face with barter media buying, but you should know that it exists and can be a very important part of the buying process for some clients.

Print Production

Why, you say, put in anything about production? Surely every agency must have someone who's familiar with all the steps in ordering and supervising to get your advertisement in print. True enough, but I want to mention some things agencies have done to improve their efficiency and make some extra money in the process. Three come readily to mind.

Stat Machines

While office copying machines have replaced photostats for many purposes, the photostat still plays an important role in advertising production because of its ability to be enlarged or reduced to almost any degree desired, all the while resulting in a sharp, glossy print suitable for reproduction. For this reason, agencies still consume amazing quantities of photostats in the normal process of producing ads. Normally these are bought from outside suppliers and clients are accustomed to being billed for them, plus, of course, your normal markup.

Some agencies I know have seen this as a profit opportunity and have installed their own stat machines. They still bill for stats at the going commercial rate, including the markup in the price, but now the agency pockets the full price not just the markup.

This gives you a more efficient operation, too. You can get your stats almost immediately. Also, if you're working late or on a Sunday to complete an important job, you can get the stats you need when you need them. You save time and annoyance and make money while doing it. Nice work if you can get it—and you can!

Typesetting

There are available small desk-top models of typesetting machines that some agencies are using very effectively. There are two basic types. One uses cold type and the other a photographic process. Both are used to set headlines and body copy. The photographic type has more flexibility in that it can scale type up or down, which allows much greater latitude in designing an ad.

Regardless of the kind of machine used, the agency can achieve all the efficiencies resulting from in-house operations and bill the client for the finished output. Like the photostat machine, this typesetting function can be a money maker as well.

Video Cameras

At least one agency I know makes very good use of a portable video camera in making presentations to its clients and also to make tapes the client can use for presentations to his sales staff. If the camera work is well done, it can even be incorporated directly in commercials. Again, as in the case of photostat and typesetting machines, the output of the video camera can be a source of profit to the agency.

Research

Do agencies need research? They can't succeed without it. No matter what you call it, it makes all the difference between seeing where you're going and flying blind. Don't fall into the common error of thinking research is only for the big shops, that smaller ones can do all right without it.

Actually the first move for an advertising person in tackling a selling problem for a client is research. The moment you look at any product or service whose sales you hope to increase, you must begin to ask questions about it, and you are up to your ears in research before you know it. Who uses the product or service? We must know this accurately before we can do any planning involving the media we will use and the message we will prepare. Where are these people? What are they like? How long have they used the product and why? What other products are there that they may use instead? What features of the product are in its favor, which are against it? What is its history? Has it been increasingly successful, or is it going downhill? Is it making or losing money? If the latter, what can be done about it? Is it a lost cause or is there hope?

These are the sort of questions that automatically should arise in the mind of any able advertising person tackling a job. There is nothing esoteric or mysterious about them. They are simply questions that should occur to any good businessperson as he or she makes plans for the promotion of any product or service. So, most research is based on just good common sense.

Often the client supplies the agency with information about the product's history, its market, and its basic character. The agency assumes the information is reliable, brushes off its own responsibility with, "that's up to the client," and plunges ahead. This can be very dangerous especially in these days when agencies have been held liable for erroneous advertising and haven't been able to get off the hook by saying, "We got the information from the client."

The best policy seems to be for the agency to decide how much market and product information is needed, and then to find out how much of this information is available in the client's own organization. Unless this is done, the agency may duplicate efforts being made elsewhere.

Does this mean that an agency must have a research department? Not at all. I think the agency's responsibility is to be research-minded and sufficiently experienced to be able to ask the right questions and properly interpret the answers. You can always buy investigative work from outside sources when needed, or have your own creative people ask questions in the field. This can help them in their creative planning too. So, if a client requires it, set up a research department, but in any event keep a positive attitude towards research as one of your tools.

Who pays for research? The best general answer would seem to be the one who benefits most. If the research is to give the agency background information for choosing the proper copy appeal, or if it's intended to help select the most efficient media to carry the message, the agency should pay for it. On the other hand, if it concerns the client's product, its characteristics, its distribution, its appeal to buyers, in short the kind of information the client should be expected to know, the client should pay. Regardless of the decision, it's vitally important that an agreement be reached about payment before any research is undertaken. To do anything else is to ask for trouble.

Traffic Control

At what point in an agency's growth does it need a special department to oversee the movement of copy and materials to meet closing dates without confusion? And, in general, how does the agency go about it?

The need for a special traffic department or individual, as is usually the case, can't be related to any set point in the growth of an agency's billings. Often a small agency will need traffic control sooner than a larger one. It depends upon the number of advertisements under preparation at any one time. An agency handling a large number of industrial accounts, for example, may need traffic control before a larger shop handling fewer national advertisements, even though they add up to more billing.

Your traffic control operation should be capable of working with broadcast advertising as well as with print. While the things with which it is necessary to deal are quite different for print and broadcast, the basic principles on which a sound and efficient traffic control system operates are the same in both cases.

Installing and Selling Traffic Control

Management must decide, of course, when the added salary expense of a traffic specialist is justified. It's much more than a clerical job because it calls for judgment, ability to install and maintain a system, and, most of all, the executive ability to get along with people.

So, if you're going into traffic control at all, better figure on a salary in the junior executive range, plus whatever office space and equipment may be needed. It won't be a negligible expense.

Once you've decided, the first step is selling the traffic system and the individual who heads it to all those in the shop with whom he or she will come in contact. No traffic control can succeed without management backing and the hearty cooperation of all agency people.

A good chief executive can easily point out to all concerned that traffic control saves time and money all along the line since it works to avoid last minute rushes, overtime work, and the inevitable errors that go along with hurried preparations for producing advertising.

What Kind of Person Do You Need?

Aside from the ability to get along with people, a successful traffic director needs to be systematic, exact, farsighted, and possessed of a considerable knowledge of all the processes that go into the preparation of advertising in all types of media. A good traffic person should know not only who does each part of a job but how it is done. He or she needs to know how long it takes to produce each element that goes into each job.

You may ask why a traffic director should have to know all these things? Isn't it enough if the production people are familiar with the technical details? No. Unless the traffic person knows exactly what he or she is asking for in the way of deliveries of art, copy, and other materials needed by a definite due date, he or she will ask for the impossible or underestimate the time required to do a job. Soon his or her credibility and authority disappears, people discount the time estimates and relapse into the previous system of getting the most urgent things out first and putting off to the last possible moment the completion of other jobs.

A prime requirement for a good traffic director is a mixture of tact and resolution. He or she has to ride herd on a temperamental bunch of account people and copy and art producers, he or she must make sure of getting his or her stuff when it's needed, and all this must be done without stepping on too many toes. Lacking authority and tact, a traffic director can create a surprising amount of resentment.

The traffic controller must know just when he or she needs whatever is asked for. Whatever date is set, he or she must stick to it, and must have the necessary experience in production to be able to explain the reason for the selected dates.

Inevitably in an agency of any size, people will be found who will do their jobs on time, accurately and to everybody's satisfaction, and others who are always trying to catch up with themselves, about to do this or that, or busy with something else of prime importance that must be done before the required job is delivered. These people, otherwise able and valuable, must be handled with tact but also with firmness. Traffic control must control; otherwise it isn't worth the money it costs.

To show what I mean, one of the most efficient traffic operations I've seen is in an Oregon agency whose traffic manager is a woman who once was a sergeant in the Air Force. Tactful, but no nonsense!

What Are the Best Control Techniques?

This is a question that can't be answered categorically. Some traffic managers work best with an elaborate wall chart, posted where all may examine it, showing clearly the status of each advertisement in process of preparation. It shows the dates for completion of each stage and provides for showing when each part has actually been completed. Other traffic managers find it easier to work with filing or loose-leaf systems on which the necessary control information is recorded.

Whatever the mechanics of the traffic control system, there are two principles that must be followed.

The essence of traffic control on any given job is to work backwards from closing dates. Determine the normal time required for each step — art, copy, production, and the like — needed to complete the job. List these with added time between steps for internal and client OK, add them all up and work back from the closing date to see when you have to start the job. In developing this schedule, of course, the traffic manager must work very closely with creative and production people and outside suppliers so all can accept the timetable as realistic.

Once you've worked this out, you'd do well to make up a standard timetable and distribute it to all account people so they won't make promises to the client they can't keep. Creative and production people should get copies too so they can know what's being promised in the way of completion dates. A typical timetable for magazine ads might look like this:

Print Timetable (Working Days)	Black & White	Two Color	Four Color
Copy and Layout	6	6	8
Estimate	1	1	1
Internal OK	2	2	2
Artwork	5	7	10
Internal OK	2	2	2
Production	6	9	20
Internal OK	2	2	2
Shipping	2	2	2
Total	26	31	47

(Note: To these figures must be added a provision for the time needed to send this ad to the client and get his approval.)

This is intended only to illustrate the principle because the time needed to complete different steps will vary widely from city to city and agency to agency. So check your local situation first but, once you've done so, draw up and distribute your timetable and insist that it be followed in scheduling your work flow.

The second basic principle is that the traffic manager must keep accurate and complete records on the jobs in the shop. He or she must know where each stage of each job is supposed to be and where it actually is. When can the next person due to work on it expect it, so he or she can plan his or her work? Is a bottleneck developing that can be corrected by changing job assignments? Does it look as though an extension may be needed? Will overtime have to be authorized? An adequate record system administered by a knowledgeable traffic manager will anticipate these questions and plan corrective action before a crisis develops.

From all this you can see that a properly organized and operated traffic control system can result in substantial dollar savings to the agency and its clients. It also can go a long way towards enhancing the agency's reputation for operating in a businesslike manner and getting work out on time with a minimum of headaches.

═ 18 ═

Public Relations

Most agencies, particularly smaller ones, think of public relations as a vague term covering advice responding to questions on company policy affecting popularity, implemented by nothing more than some perfunctory releases — informative material more or less well done that, it is optimistically hoped, will get itself published for free. Once the stuff has been sent on its way to the editorial trash basket, most agencies do nothing more to see what happened to it. But public relations is far more than that!

What Public Relations Is

While advertising is mostly concerned with what makes people buy, public relations goes much further into the wide range of human opinions, prejudices, likes and dislikes — motivation, if you will. It requires the nicest possible understanding of what makes people think and act as they do. It involves favorable contacts between the advertiser and the individuals and companies with whom it does business.

A company's public relations department looks both inward and outward. It examines the company's employees from bottom to top and endeavors to find out what will make them work most effectively. From there it spreads outward to vendors who sell to the company and to all who have anything to do with the distribution of its goods or services. Still further out, it encompasses consumers. Are they pleased, satisfied, or unhappy? Are they vulnerable to the inroads of competitors? Are they likely to stay customers of the company or would only a small inducement swing them over into another camp?

How about legislators whose decisions may affect the advertiser's fortunes favorably or adversely? Do they know and like the company? Are they armed in advance against unfavorable rumors or inspired releases from competitors?

How about the media that are read by individuals whose good opinion is desired? Are they in possession of all pertinent facts about the advertiser's product or service? If a possible purchaser should ask for an opinion from their editors, would it be favorable?

Public relations work, then, means shaping the policies that affect standing, credit, and reputation. It means building a backlog of favorable bias. It means adding the plus, however intangible, that gives the company possessing it a better break against competition. It should make higher prices, where they are deserved, accepted without rancor.

The Role of the Agency

I doubt that any agency can serve its client properly without being vitally interested in the advertiser's public relations. When the client has his or her own public relations department, or when an able and accredited public relations firm or individual is employed, the agency should help all it can, without criticism. But failing the presence of an experienced public relations advisor, the agency either should advise the employment of one or become such itself.

To do this takes time and money, but often it is worth it. The agency must become familiar with many relationships far beyond those usually considered as advertising or even marketing. It must build such confidence on the client's part that even unfavorable judgments, sometimes reflecting on the client's efficiency, may be offered safely and with some chance of adoption without hurt feelings.

The timing of establishing this new and desirable relationship between client and agency is important. You don't start out by saying, "This is a new kind of arrangement, one in which we are going to do more for you, and you are going to pay us what we deserve." You must establish your value first. You must demonstrate that you have the business judgment to guide the client toward successful performance in his or her internal and external communications with all individuals and corporations in situations that affect his or her welfare.

In the mind of the advertiser you become primarily a business counselor. A good public relations advisor, in the agency or outside of it, is a prime builder and guardian of a company's reputation. No service is more important than this.

I believe that any agency, large or small, that is capable of giving its clients good business advice, which it may sell under the familiar term "public relations," will have little trouble in holding its business and being paid properly for its services.

How do you get paid for this kind of service? Invariably it is by a fee of some sort. One common method is to charge a monthly retainer that establishes the client as a regular customer entitled to seek advice from you whenever he or she wants. When advice is sought, you charge for whatever time your people spend on the job. Be sure you charge for every hour spent and that your rates cover your direct costs, including overhead, plus a profit.

But make sure that the individuals concerned know their business and are clearly worth what they get. Don't send a child to do an adult's work. Nowhere does ineptitude show up more quickly than in this difficult job. Nowhere can the agency damage its own standing faster. If you can't do it right, duck it completely and advise the employment of someone who can.

One delightful difference between an advertising account and a public relations account is that the latter starts generating income the minute the agency starts working with the client. If your agreement calls for starting on the 15th of February, say, your first bill to the client is for the retainer for the last half of February, usually rendered in advance.

Contrast this with an advertising account also signed up on February 15th. In this case, you start writing copy, making layouts, and selecting media. Then comes production to get the message into the media. Finally, you bill the client and get your payment. This whole process can take three to four months. So it may be May or June before you receive a cent in income and all this time you've been paying salaries and other expenses. Quite a plus for public relations.

=19==

Inside, Outside, or Some of Each

With all the functions an agency performs for its clients, how do you organize for greatest efficiency? There are a lot of different ways. Often a single agency uses more than one; in other instances an agency progresses from one to another as it grows; still other agencies perform some services internally and buy others from outside specialists.

Doing It Yourself

By "doing it yourself" I mean performing all, or almost all, functions internally with your own staff. It is still the basic concept on which most agencies operate, but with variations. Here are some of them.

The Jack-of-All-Trades Approach
The agency just starting out almost has to adopt this approach simply because it doesn't have a big enough staff to allow specialization. Even as an agency grows, however, it frequently makes sense to confer the responsibility for more than one function on one person.

Copy-contact is probably the most common example of this kind of organization. It finds its most frequent use on industrial accounts in which the account executive may personally write the copy. For this type of client the copy is usually highly technical. It's much more efficient if, when the client feels some change is needed, the account executive can make it on the spot instead of having to go back to the agency, explain the changes to a copywriter, and then have to take the revised copy back to the client. This functional organization is used frequently even in large diversified agencies that may set up a separate department to handle industrial clients on this basis.

Media   is often added to the responsibilities of the account executive. Again this is usually done in the case of industrial accounts in which the proper selection of media depends more on knowledge of the impact different publications will have on technical-minded groups than it does on highly sophisticated media analysis techniques.

Groups or Departments?

This question usually arises in connection with the organization of the creative function. The followers of the group concept set up creative groups each of which may consist of one or more writers and one or more artists. They always work as a group and thus bring a total creative approach to the client's problems. Such a group may work with a single account executive and thus constitute almost a separate small agency within the whole agency. If significant broadcast advertising is involved, the group may be expanded to include an expert in broadcast production.

At the other extreme is strict departmental organization where a job is turned over to the art department or the copy department and assigned to any one of a number of people. The department head will probably try to assign the same client's work to the same person at all times, but the basic philosophy is that all staff members are generalists who should be able to work on any kind of problem.

Which type of organization an agency adopts will depend on how technical its clients' problems are and on the personalities of its staff—whether they are team players or individualists.

Modules

The ultimate expression of departmental organization is the agency that operates on the modular principle. In this case the different functions are organized as separate profit centers with almost complete autonomy. An agency offers clients the use of as many of these modular services as it wishes with no utilization of, or charge for, functions not used. An à la carte menu, if you will.

In addition, the modular agency can offer one or more specific services to advertisers who are not regular clients. Many agencies operate in this manner. Among the services offered by agencies I know are media buying, media analysis, broadcast production, photographic studio services, public relations, and yellow page and other directory advertising. If one looked hard enough, it's quite likely that every agency service except client contact could be bought à la carte from some agency somewhere.

Buying It Outside

Some of the agency services I've been talking about have always been available from outside sources. Public relations is a good example; art studios are another. Almost every agency will buy at least its finished art from outside studios if for no other reason than because it can't afford to keep a whole staff of artists continually occupied, with all the different skills and techniques its clients need. Many agencies, especially the smaller ones, will even have rough layouts made on the outside.

There are also quite a few "boutiques" that specialize in the written part of the creative package. These sell their talents on a project basis for a fee based on the time used or on a retainer basis. This plan gives the agency a call on their services up to a specified maximum in a given period of time. Some of these establishments also offer art services so they can perform the whole creative function if desired.

Another group of shops specializes in broadcast advertising. Most of these are purely production houses and thus perform services that most agencies would never perform internally in any event. Some of them, however, also include the writing function and hence properly fall in the boutique category.

Another service that can be purchased from outside sources is research. Like broadcast specialists, research firms are normally considered outside suppliers, but in some cases they, too, can take on attributes of a boutique to supplement the agency's own department.

Probably the most notable increase in the number of these outside services has been in the media field. Most of these companies started out as buying services and many still limit themselves to that function. Others have expanded to the point where they can serve as a complete media department. This service runs the whole gamut from developing objectives and strategy, through buying space or time, to approving the media invoices and paying the media.

Some of Each

Some agencies are organized to perform all the normal services internally, but even these agencies will use the boutiques from time to time. Maybe they have an unexpectedly heavy work load and need some help; maybe they want outside thinking as a sort of brainstorming session to inspire their own people.

Other agencies prefer not to increase their staff to perform all the agency functions themselves. They feel it's more efficient to provide broad supervision for the media buying function, for example, but have an outside service handle all the details.

Still others mix things up even more and use outside services for some clients but not for others. So the existence of these boutiques gives the agency flexibility in meeting the needs of clients. The smart agency principal is constantly aware of sources of help and what sort of help he or she can expect. It may not be needed often, but it can be a lifesaver.

Agency Networks

How many agency networks are there? What size and kind of agencies join them? How useful are they? What do they cost?

When the first edition of this book was published in 1964 it listed seven networks with "an eighth, it is reported, in process of organization." These seven listed 196 member agencies. There are now nine active networks with some 360 member agencies in the United States. Here they are, listed in order of founding, with an approximate count of members according to a July 1985 article in *Advertising Age:*

1932 AMIN Advertising & Marketing Network, Stamford, Connecticut, 58 Members

1932 NAAN National Advertising Agency Network, New York, New York, 50 Members

1938 AAAI Affiliated Advertising Agencies International, Aurora, Colorado, 72 Members

1938 TAAN Transworld Advertising Agency Network, Englewood, Colorado, 25 Members

1946 MAAN Mutual Advertising Agency Network, Detroit, Michigan, 30 Members

1950 IFAA International Federation of Advertising Agencies, Sarasota, Florida, 50 Members

1961 ICITA International Chain of Industrial and Technical Advertising Agencies, Cincinnati, Ohio, 44 Members

1968 IAAA Intermarket Association of Advertising Agencies, Dayton, Ohio, 20 Members

1980 MAN Midstates Agency Network, Cleveland, Ohio, 12 Members

What kind of agencies join networks? Well, almost any kind. Some specialize in a certain kind of client or industry while others have very broad interests. In size they range from billings of approximately $1.2 million to $235 million according to their listings in the *Standard Register of Advertising Agencies*. This equates to about $240,000 to $47 million in gross income.

How do networks operate? Following the principles laid down by Lynn W. Ellis, originator of the network concept, each of them is a voluntary affiliation of independent advertising agencies closely cooperating, chiefly by resident principals, to provide nationwide or even international service in line with the trend toward intensive localization of marketing campaigns. Originally all of them operated internally through the voluntary efforts of their members, but the trend is now to a more professional approach that finds most of them with permanent, full-time paid managers.

How much do networks cost? Annual dues are usually based on the size of the agency member and can run from a low of about $100 to a high of $3,500. In addition, there are the expenses of attending meetings (usually two or three) held each year. The expense of attending meetings can bring the total cost of membership into the area of $10,000 per year.

How can you benefit from network membership? Chiefly from access to a truly limitless source of information and help for you and your clients based on intimate local knowledge. A cardinal principle on which all networks operate is that there is not more than one member in any market, hence members don't compete with each other. So the interchange of information is free and uninhibited; questions on even the most sensitive subjects are asked—and answered—with no holds barred. In answer to questions like, "You have a savings and loan account; what appeals have you found most effective in attracting new accounts from young married people? What media mix is most effective in reaching them?" you'll get not only tear sheets, storyboards, media schedules, and costs, but an evaluation of the results obtained. Try that one on Madison Avenue.

Information also is exchanged on all manner of subjects relating to agency operations. What do you bill for? What kind of markups do you use? What's your most effective new business technique? How do you compensate your account executives? And so on.

Probably the ultimate in useful advice from one network member to another is that which results in the acquisition of a new account. Network headquarters files are full of examples of this kind of thing. Here's a specific documented example with only the names changed.

Joe, the president of an agency located in one of the Mountain states heard that a manufacturer of outdoor sports clothing and equipment was about to select an agency. The manufacturer was well-known locally and apparently was prepared to spend enough money to give the agency a gross income in excess of $75,000. Very tempting, but Joe really didn't know beans about this particular industry. So what did he do?

From information available from his network, Joe learned that Dick, another network member located on the West Coast, had a lot of experience and current clients in this same industry. So, Joe got hold of Dick and was thoroughly briefed on the peculiarities of the outdoor sports business, the factors that made for success or failure, the kind of customers to seek, and how best to appeal to them.

What happened? When Joe made his presentation to the prospect, it immediately became apparent that he'd done his homework. He knew, and showed he knew, where the customers were, how to reach them, and how to speak the language of the trade. This headstart made such an impression on the prospect that Joe got the account.

Of course, this kind of thing doesn't happen every day but, if you're successful in pulling it off only once, your network dues has paid for itself for many years to come.

As for service to you and your clients based on intimate local knowledge of the market, a recent example will make clear what can be done. An East Coast network member writes his client, "Yesterday, one of the ads we received from you was for placement in Dallas this weekend. In checking our data file, we found that Dallas has two Sunday papers . . . their circulation equal (within 800 copies, believe it or not) . . . and their rates are exactly the same. We were told to pick the best one, which, on paper, seemed like the flip of a coin. We called our Dallas network affiliate asking their recommendation. Turns out that the *Dallas News* is vastly superior for classified help wanted—a fact only a local would know. No extra charge!"

A complaint frequently heard is that the job of an agency president is one of the loneliest in the world because you don't have anyone with whom to discuss your problems. Not so for members of networks. At regular meetings there are innumerable opportunities to talk face to face with your peers about your common problems and with members from 15 or 20 states covering the width and breadth of the country; the wealth of information and diversity of viewpoints available is tremendous.

With members from large metropolitan areas, important regional centers, and small towns you get the benefit of the thinking of all kinds of agency people, not just the denizens of Madison and Michigan Avenues. What's more, these people are intimately involved in the day-to-day operations of their agencies and know firsthand the virtues of living within one's income and putting aside a bit for a rainy day.

With almost no large national accounts in which domination by size, color, or frequency of insertion seems to be the name of the game, network principals are up to their ears in industrial advertising, in local television shows, in couponed advertising, in direct mail—those areas of advertising in which the expenditure has to bring home the bacon, or else. As a result, they have a keen understanding of their value to clients and are not afraid to charge accordingly.

In recent years there have been a few instances of a network handling a national account—usually structured by having one member act as the flagship agency responsible for basic planning and the creative concept with outlying member agencies providing local knowledge of media, merchandising, and the like, and doing most of the local and regional contact and promotion. The number of individual members involved with any such client depends on their location in relation to the client's distribution patterns.

Once networks are mentioned, a frequent question is, "I'm a member of AAAA so why do I need a network?" Actually the two organizations complement, rather than compete with, each other. The personalized, noncompetitive help available to network members has already been described. AAAA can't foster this kind of interchange of sensitive information because, with many members in the same city, its members are bound to be in competition with each other and hence understandably reluctant to speak out freely.

On the other hand, AAAA is the national spokesman for the industry and its members handle about 75 percent of all advertising placed through agencies. Hence it can supply industry-wide statistics; maintain a comprehensive library on advertising subjects; keep its members advised about governmental and other regulations and taxes affecting advertising; and make available all kinds of group insurance plans that much smaller networks cannot equal. The noncompeting nature of AAAA and the networks is best demonstrated by the fact that in 1972 more than 25 percent of network members also belonged to AAAA. By 1986 this percentage had increased to 47 percent.

V New Business— The Lifeblood of an Agency

=21=

Locating Your Prospects

Like Hamlet, advertising agencies are particularly likely to "suffer the slings and arrows of outrageous fortune," the losses of income that are completely beyond their control. Clients reduce their advertising budgets but not their needs for service; they are acquired by or merged with other advertisers; they may move out of town. All this is in addition to losses of income from attrition, that is, clients seeking greener pastures elsewhere.

So, an agency constantly must be involved in seeking new business as a simple matter of survival.

Also, most agencies want to keep their staff members together and productive and they can't do that unless they recognize and reward their individual hopes for the future. To do this requires a dynamic and growing agency, which means new business.

These two overriding reasons—survival and the need to grow—dictate that an agency's top management must consider new business one of its primary responsibilities and must organize to seek it. New business seldom just falls in your lap. You have to work for it.

Good as your agency may be, prospects have to be constantly and convincingly told about it. It's fine to build a better mousetrap, but don't let anybody fool you with that old story about the world beating a path to your door. Put the trap on display and have a mouse in it, at that.

Who Are Your Prospects and Where Are They?

No doubt about it, your best new business prospects are your present clients. You know them and they know you. Presumably you're doing a good job for them or you'd have been replaced already. If you're doing a good job for them, their sales will grow and, as a result, their advertising expenditures will probably expand. They may be opening up new territories. They may be bringing out new products or buying companies in related lines of business. Because you know these people you've got the inside track.

When you look beyond your present clients, start with a market survey. The need for this is as evident in new business work as in all other phases of the selling job for clients. The product you seek to sell is your agency. Who will buy it, where are they, in what lines of business, and how large are they? These questions concerning the market for your own product must be answered carefully.

In general, an agency is best at soliciting lines they know something about or for which they have an affinity. The shop wastes time if it pitches for accounts that are too large for it to handle, or are located too far away. It's fine to be optimistic, but it's better to be realistic. Also, the number of accounts to be solicited should be small, the effort intensive rather than extensive. Concentrating on a few really possible prospects will pay off better than spreading the butter too thin. Let's look separately at some of these considerations.

Industry

First, concentrate on industries in which you have experience, either directly or in closely related fields. If you've handled bank advertising it's not too far a cry to go after savings and loan companies; advertising an industrial pump is not too different from an electric motor, but experience with either would mean little to an advertiser of package goods sold to housewives.

When adding up your experiences, don't overlook what your people may have done before they came to you. Get each of them to list all industries they've been involved with and you may be surprised at the number of industries covered. Americans are a highly mobile people both geographically and job-wise and unexpected talents turn up all over the place.

Geography

Modern travel is fast—you know, breakfast in London, lunch in New York, dinner in San Francisco (don't try doing it in reverse!)—but also expensive. So, keep both time and expense of travel in mind when thinking about soliciting out-of-town prospects.

It's quite common to do as one Midwestern agency does. It limits its new business efforts to cities that can be reached in an hour by air from its headquarters city. But geography can be a positive factor as well. Look at the kind of approach a Mountain states agency took.

One of this agency's largest clients is a local bank. When bank holding companies began to proliferate, this client formed one and acquired local banks all over its state. The agency had to visit each of these outlying banks at regular intervals, which began to take a lot of time and money. So the agency made a virtue out of necessity and started actively soliciting new clients in the cities where the local banks were. As a result it obtained more clients and was able to service several on each trip.

Another agency, in San Francisco, does the same thing on a local basis. It tries to concentrate on prospects that are located in the same industrial park as one of its present clients so that one call can cover several bases at once.

Size

Size works two ways. First, don't bite off more than you can chew. Big accounts are fine but not if they are so large in relation to the size of the agency that they can't be handled without seriously reducing the amount and quality of service to other clients. Well, you may say, why not staff up to handle the new account? This is fine up to a point, but you can't service an important account with all new people. You've got to have a nucleus of tried and trusted people who can provide the necessary direction and adherence to your standards of quality and service.

At the other extreme are very small accounts. These can chew up a lot of staff time while producing very little income. It's tempting to take on accounts like these that can provide incremental income with no addition to staff but it can become a trap that results in limiting or reducing service to other clients. If a small account has real potential to develop, by all means take it on as an investment in the future. But watch it carefully and don't stick with it if it becomes apparent that the potential isn't going to develop.

Who Should Work on New Business?

Two agencies I know answer this question simply, if not simplistically. One, in Missouri, tells its people "New business is your business"; the other, in Wisconsin, says "New business is everybody's business." No doubt both of these statements point up the vital role new business activity plays in an agency's scheme of things, but they hardly represent a sound blueprint for organizing the new business function.

The ideal new business setup within the agency is a separate department headed by an individual skilled in agency selling. This, however, is completely impractical except for the largest shops. Small agencies cannot afford the salary burden of individuals who perform only the soliciting function. The results are almost invariably too uncertain and too far off in time.

In small agencies, new business responsibility must be assumed by the principals. Theoretically, they should allocate a substantial part of their time (some say as much as a third) to seeking new billing to replace that which is normally lost, to provide growth, and to insure the future of their business. But you know how it is: clients and service first, new business when you have time or when you're clearly in trouble.

So for the smaller shops, the solution would be to name a seasoned executive of management stature to head a New Business Committee as a permanent assignment. This need not be a full-time job, but the executive, with the help of a capable assistant, should build a card file of suitable prospects of a size, character, and location the agency could profitably serve.

The new-business person should assign suitable people to contact each of the names on this list, preferably about once a month. Then he or she should make sure the results of each contact are carefully noted on the card so the record will always be complete.

As you can see, this way of going after new business is far from automatic. It requires man or woman power constantly and consistently used with intelligence and adaptability. Delegate certain suitable persons to spend part time on this work, but see that the time is allocated and used because agencies now know that getting new business is not simply desirable, it is essential. Either you grow or you are on the way out in this business.

Definite time allocated and personal contacts with prospects—that's the formula, and the only one that works.

22
Approaching Your Prospects

You can have the best list of prospects in the world—one that is right as to industry, location, and size—but as long as they're just sitting out there somewhere, they're not going to become clients. You have to make contact with them, get them enough interested in you and your agency to give you a hearing, and then sell them your services. This chapter will discuss the first of these steps.

The First Approach to a Prospect

Once your prospect list has been refined, how do you make your approach? I'm talking about the steps that precede a face-to-face meeting. There are three basic means of communication—personalized letters, the telephone, and direct-mail campaigns to a selected mailing list.

Personalized Letters

Advertisers are interested primarily in their own businesses so the more your sales letter can concentrate on the prospect's business, rather than on extolling your agency's capabilities, the better. If you can go even further toward personalization by addressing the prospect by his or her first name (as can be done in many smaller cities), so much the better.

If you're not on a first-name basis with the prospect, a letter like this addressed to the president of the prospective client can be an excellent door-opener:

Dear Mr. Jones:

We plan, within the next several months, to solicit your advertising account.

This, because we know and like your field, and specifically your company, and are experienced in the food [substitute appropriate word] business. We shall send you, from time to time, items of information we have gathered that we believe will be of use to you. We may even be rash enough to suggest selling or marketing procedures which seem to us, looking in from the outside, as likely to improve your sales and/or profit picture. We figure, if there is any chance of our doing business together, this is the best way to turn a possibility into a fact.

Sincerely yours,
(Agency head)

This letter will bear careful analysis. You will note it does not ask for an answer, but it is highly likely to get one, if only, "We can't stop you." Only if the possibility of a client-agency relationship is entirely out will the advertiser write and say so, in which event the prospect will be removed from the solicitation list. In general, the letter presents the advertising agency in a most desirable light, interested primarily in the prosperity and progress of the client, and planning to do what it can from the outside, to promote these ends.

The success of this agency's new business program, launched so modestly yet with such precision, depends on what it digs up and passes on to the prospect in the way of suggestions and advice.

Send the prospect material applicable to his company alone, and be sure to make the material look natural and not contrived. One great way to do this involves the use of the candid camera. Take photographs of the prospect's own merchandise being bought and used; then send them to him. Nothing, but nothing, as Gimbels says, will hit the advertiser harder. It absolutely guarantees favorable attention.

Suppose you want to add a food account to your billing, and ten advertisers in this category are represented in your nearby supermarket. One day's work by a skilled photographer with a fast 35mm camera should give you candid shots of all ten food producers' merchandise, on the shelves, under consideration by shoppers, in the carts, and on the checkout counters.

The Telephone
The art of telephone solicitation is still so much in its infancy that I'm sure you will welcome some suggestions on how to handle it. These will be old

hat to the telephone people, who have been training their personnel along these lines for so long with such signal success. The average businessperson, however, still needs telephone training.

First, a few fundamentals. Remember, "The Voice with the Smile Wins"? Never, but never, use anyone in telephone solicitations except a person with a pleasant, easily understood voice, and a personality such as that type of voice expresses.

The next fundamental is psychological. Most phone solicitations are cold turkey, without even your personal presence to help break down the bars. Into the privacy of a person's business office comes a completely strange voice (one assumes you have been smart enough to get by the guardian secretary), and this voice starts right in talking about a matter on which the recipient has, probably, no desire to talk.

More often than most of us realize, this strange voice is not easily understood, and the conversation gets off on the wrong foot with "Who is this? What do you want to talk to me about?" and "Sorry, I don't understand you." All this is very, very bad. Worse, far worse, than if you hadn't made contact with your prospect at all.

Bearing these horrible pitfalls in mind, here is an example of a proper approach. Speaking slowly and distinctly, say: "Mr. Jones, thank you for letting me talk with you. This is Jim Smith. I'm with the XYZ Advertising Agency in (city). In one of our marketing operations recently, we encountered your product under such-and-such circumstances. (Here utilize a price situation, a competitive operation, a store promotion, or whatever else you have dug up. Be sure it is authentic, new, and of some importance.) We have an idea that grew out of this situation. May I come to see you about it?"

In this approach, notice 1. your disarming and courteous thanks for the prospect's time, 2. your clear identification, with no attempt at camouflage, 3. your immediate mention of a possible idea of value applicable to his or her business, and 4. your direct request for an appointment on a business matter of legitimate importance.

This is the type of approach that almost invariably pulls a friendly response from the prospect. This response will vary all the way from "Sorry, not a chance" to "All right, we're not changing agencies, you understand, but we never refuse to listen to anyone who can help us build our business." Which, at this stage of the game, is tops in success.

I can't remember how many times I've telephoned, cold turkey, to presidents of multimillion dollar corporations using this direct and sincere approach, to be met often with a hearty "Thank God for a guy who wants my business and has guts enough to ask for it." You know, the bigger they are, the easier they are to approach, provided you speak their language. If you don't, you usually won't even get past the switchboard operator.

Other Methods

Far behind the personalized letter and the telephone, in my opinion, are the multitude of other devices agencies use to make a favorable first impression on a prospect that they hope will lead to a face-to-face meeting. Some agencies buy syndicated newsletters with their own selling message on the back; others send out expensive proofs of some of their ads; some use elaborate printed matter.

Then there are the various forms of house organs agencies write and distribute. With few exceptions, however, these are not too useful because, editorially speaking, most agencies aren't skilled enough to turn out a really effective house organ.

Be Persistent

Constant, consistent, and continuous effort is the key to success. Letters, which usually are the most effective and economical initial communication, should go out at least once a month, and for a much longer period than most agencies realize. Over and over again, a letter series has brought response after a couple of years of hammering. It's pretty certain that nothing much will happen fast, unless you get an exceedingly good break, so you must prepare yourself for a long and weary path.

It is not advisable to push too hard for responses at first, although later it may be very good practice to enclose a return postcard asking politely, "Shall we keep it up, or would you rather we'd turn it off?" But avoid digging up the seeds to see how the garden is doing.

Whom Do You Contact?

One of the most valuable new business tools your agency can have is a card file listing every prospect you've selected as being right for you based on industry, location, and size. The card for each prospect should show the name and title of all persons who would have any influence on decisions concerning advertising. Obviously the list must be kept up to date because you won't make a favorable impression by addressing a person with last year's title.

The person you're most interested in reaching is the one who can really make the decisions on advertising. Chance are, in most cases, it's not the ad manager.

If the prospect got on your list as a result of a tip from a media rep, for instance, he can probably tell you who the real decision maker is. If you don't know for sure, go down the list of officers, pick out the most likely people, and send them all individual letters. There is no objection to sending the same letter to several people in one organization. You are communicating what you have on your mind and the more individuals you can talk to about the subject, the better. (Barring clear indications to the contrary, always include the president on your list.)

As soon as such a program has started, certain individuals will emerge from the anonymity of the list into the definite classification of "interested, mildly or more, or at least willing to be shown." These people are the ones on whom you concentrate.

The First Meeting

Once you perceive any indication of interest from a prospect, get on the phone and make an appointment to see him or her. This gives you the opportunity to present your wares in a favorable atmosphere. What do you show the prospect? Every agency has its own favorite technique.

A Michigan agency has prepared a series of booklets, each concerning an industry with which the agency has a successful track record. Each includes samples of ads, brochures, releases, and case histories of actual work for clients in the particular industry. The appropriate ones are discussed in detail with the prospect.

A Massachusetts agency uses a variation of this plan. Each year it routinely reviews the plans drawn up for each client and the ways in which the agency has implemented them. This is all reduced to written form and, if the client and prospect are noncompetitive, shown to the prospect and discussed at length. This same agency gives prospects a complete list of its clients and includes the name of the people with whom the agency deals. The agency man leaves the list with the prospect saying, "These people are my best salespeople; call them up and ask about my agency."

A Pennsylvania agency regularly prepares a portfolio of print ads and tapes of broadcasts that they feel represent their best work. These are shown to prospects not just as samples of work, but as solutions to problems. The examples are tailored for each important prospect and tend to include ads with wide exposure in the prospect's area. The reaction they're looking for is a statement from the prospect like, "Yeah, I remember that ad. Did you make it?"

This first personal contact is also a good opportunity to trot out some facts you've learned about the prospect's products. But be sure you know what you're talking about and be extremely careful to present these facts modestly, unassumingly, and tactfully.

The essence of this approach is that it is definite, aimed at the improvement of a situation that really exists, and that it is the best possible showcase of the agency's abilities. If they can talk like this from the outside, reasons the prospect, they certainly ought to be able to help us a lot once they are working with us. The agency is careful not to spell this out. Any good businessperson can reason from facts given him, and he doesn't have to have his nose rubbed in them.

The more you can talk informedly about the prospect's business, the better off you will be. Nothing interests a person as much as him- or herself. So a new idea is fine, provided it's good, and so are field reports, provided they're accurate. But Lord help you if your idea is unsound for his or her particular business, or if your reports have been culled from prejudiced competitors, sore salesmen, or disillusioned dealers.

23

The Formal Presentation

After the successful first approach to a prospect has resulted in one or more face-to-face meetings, the next step in a new business solicitation is usually a formal presentation.

Depending on the size of the account, one or more people represent the agency and the prospect. Thus the presentation may be anything from an across-the-desk confrontation of an agency head and the client president or owner, to a sizeable meeting of several people from the agency and a like number from the client's organization.

Whichever it is, the prime cause of success or failure is certainly psychological. Whether it is one person's or a group's reaction to what the agency has to say, it adds up to a mental impression, all the way from totally unfavorable to totally favorable. All the way from "No, out of the question" to "Yes, these people are just what we have been looking for."

Just as advertising seeks to say well what a successful personal salesman would say to a prospect face-to-face, so the agency presentation seeks to sell its people, its facilities, and its abilities.

In the final analysis what the agency is making, through its presentation, is a sale of its people. Not of buildings, or bricks and mortar, not of financial stability, not of inventories, or cash in the bank, or of facilities, although somewhere along the line these must have been given consideration. Primarily the attempted sale is one of brains, of mental compatibility, of promotional abilities, of human relations capacity, and of people.

The situation confronting the representatives of the client and of the agency forecasts the many situations that will arise as the combination of individuals begins to work together. So the more representative of the future the presentation can be, the more likely it is that the presentation will succeed and the partnership be successful.

Whatever in the presentation is psychologically sound, then, is of supreme importance. Less important are the physical details. They are more or less self-evident, anyhow: keep it simple, keep it interesting.

Who Should Make the Agency's Presentation?

The answer to this question lies in the new-business setup that the agency has constructed in advance. The thing to watch out for here is the prospect's quick suspicion and resentment if he is solicited by principals and new business specialists and then finds out that these able and articulate guys will not be in the picture at all as the account gets going. "No, our Mr. Zilch over there in the corner is the man who will serve you, with, of course, the agency heads, too, whenever they are needed." "Oh yeah? We've heard that one before!"

Definitely the individual who will serve the account, whether he is an account executive or the agency owner, should make the presentation, appear as the head honcho, the keynoter, the voice of the agency. Let him or her drag in all the associates he or she wants to: media people, researchers, specialists. Fine. But let him or her do the dragging. "This is a sample, gentlemen, of the way your account will be handled, should you elect to entrust it to us." Or, better yet, "This is the way we work, we hope you like it and can we have the business?" Just like that, if you're got this far with the prospect.

Ask for the business, right out. It can't do any harm and you might get it.

Where Should the Presentation Be Made?

There are only three possibilities—the agency's office, the client's office, or some neutral ground such as a hotel meeting room. Normally the prospect will dictate the location and the agency has no choice but to go along.

If they can swing it, however, there's a lot to be said for making the presentation in the agency's office in comfortable and familiar surroundings. This gives the prospect a chance to see the agency's facilities, meet its people, and be assured that a whole team will be working on his or her account. The fact that the prospect is going to visit the agency's office also gives a big boost to the morale of all the agency employees.

Another big plus in using the agency's office is thorough familiarity with the surroundings and the equipment available for use during the presentation. The presentation may be much more effective if made by using specialized equipment that can't be transported readily to another location. I have in mind such things as specially built simulated TV receivers on which commercials can be shown in a realistic homelike atmosphere.

If the presentation is to be made elsewhere, be sure to check it out in advance to the greatest extent possible. Know the physical surroundings, available equipment, and any limitations on its use. This will avoid disasters such as happened to one agency making a presentation in a hotel meeting room. This agency arrived with six or eight people each lugging a piece of audiovisual equipment. They started the presentation and kept adding electrical equipment as needed. Everything was going beautifully until, wham, they blew a fuse. End of presentation! Moral: check the facilities, including standbys, ahead of time.

When's the Best Time to Present?

It is physically impossible for a client to judge agency desirability properly when several meetings a day are scheduled with a dozen or more agencies that have seemed eligible to serve him. No more than one meeting a day should be planned, and no more than three in any one week. Both parties need that much time to prepare for the meetings and to digest whatever is produced in the presentations.

It is bad judgment, and bad psychology, to try to speed up the process; hurried, high-tension meetings create serious pressures. It is in the agency's best interests to resist becoming a part of any such procedure. Here, right at the beginning of the contacts between agency and prospect, the agency should make clear the need for a normal atmosphere in which to present its case. Of course, this is easier said than done. Usually the agency takes whatever situation is offered and does the best it can. But it is highly desirable, in prepresentation contacts, when the coming conference is informally discussed, that the agency make this important point.

A prospect is favorably impressed by an agency attitude that emphasizes the importance of the meeting and resists being pushed into haste or time limit restraints. All these considerations come into the psychology of the presentation. The relationship being considered by both parties needs to be entered into with care and deliberation. Only then has it a chance to become permanent and confer all the benefits it should upon both agency and client.

If a whole series of presentations is being made, as is usually the case, the agency would be wise to try to appear either first or last. The first agency to present can set the standard against which those to follow are judged; the last one to present has the last word and can shine in comparison with what has gone before. The agencies in the middle are likely to stay there.

What Should Be Included?

The main theme of any presentation should be what the agency knows best: its own abilities and accomplishments, and it should point towards its sound business judgment. The presentation should demonstrate that it knows what works.

An agency can make a most impressive presentation by assembling case histories of problems that had confronted its clients, and the professional advice that steered the advertiser along the right track. The supplementary means by which it implemented this course—the unusual approach, the marketing aids, the excellent art and copy—are all subsidiary to, and less important than, the direction indicator. Yes, as vitally important to the advertiser as the compass is to the navigator is a knowledge of what works. To the extent that they can do so, agencies should select case histories that are discernibly applicable to the prospect's needs and interests. In talking about the prospect's problems and opportunities it's important not to go out on a limb by expressing opinions off the top of one's head which the prospect may immediately recognize as unsound.

If it's handled soundly and intelligently the personalized pitch is invariably the most memorable and effective one. Remember the last word in the universal human reaction to any appeal, "What's in it for *me?*"

To close this section here is one specific "do" and one "don't."

First, the do. I firmly believe every agency presentation should include a section on agency compensation. This is the logical time to introduce this vital subject. It's far better to agree beforehand what is going to be billed to the advertiser and how, than to wait for the first bills to go to the client only to provoke questions like, "How come you bill us for layouts?" An agreement at this stage can prevent innumerable headaches and hassles later.

Second, the don't. Don't make speculative presentations unless the prospect asks for them and offers to pay for them. To follow any other course costs a lot of time and money and, more important, is highly dangerous because chances are overwhelming that such a presentation would have to be based on incomplete information.

How About Techniques?

The answer to this will have to depend on knowledge of the prospects. Some of them will want a full-scale dog and pony show; others will prefer to sit down across a desk with nothing more than a simple flip chart. Find out as much as possible about what's expected and try to comply.

Regardless of the overall form of the presentation, here are some techniques that may seem self-evident but are frequently overlooked. Your presentation should be the work of many people. The analysis should be made by analysts, the presentation should be planned by good constructive thinkers, and the actual delivery should be by a good speaker who is fast on his feet and who knows when to throw the ball to associates. This front person should avoid reading what he or she has to say; he or she should know the material so thoroughly that notes are not necessary. The points, however, should be reinforced by a visual easel presentation whose pages can be turned without looking at them too much.

The audience gets a double-strength impression when they both hear and see the points the speaker is making. Statistics, figures, territorial characteristics, and charts may be turned to and read from the easel. But don't dwell too long on this sort of thing, lest you hear a voice from the wings saying, "Work faster, kid, they're walking out on you!"

Take it easy, be informal but courteous; don't get too familiar; watch out for personal prejudices of the individuals whom you are addressing; remember not to step on the toes of the sales manager or the advertising manager, if there is one.

Talk slowly; people are often more deaf than they will admit. Be clear and simple. Avoid fireworks and forensics. Believe in what you're selling and show it in your entire attitude. Don't, for God's sake, know it all.

If your audience shows signs of going to sleep, ask questions. If you get the prospect talking, you're really cooking. Silence is all too often hostile. Feel the patient's pulse occasionally to see how he or she is doing.

Try to design a simple mnemonic device that will be useful to your audience in following the presentation as you make it. It will also serve to remind them of your agency when they're reviewing the presentations they've heard.

One of the best of these I've seen is a *score card* developed by a Missouri agency. Physically it's a printed form tailor-made for each presentation. The left-hand column is headed "Strengths You Should Want in Your Advertising Agency." Below this heading are listed the major points you plan to make in your presentation.

The sample form I have before me lists such agency strengths as steady growth, full-service capability, stature in industry, resultful creativity, media knowledge, knowledge of (prospect's name) markets and products, and best team for (prospect's name). The next column — a nice wide one — is headed by the name of your agency and in it, opposite each of the main points in the left-hand column, is a neatly printed outline of the most important things you plan to talk about.

Other columns are left blank for the prospect to take notes on what the other presenting agencies have to say on each of these major points. If you know who your competitors are going to be, it's a good idea to print their names at the head of these other columns. It shows you're on the ball and alert to your competition!

The whole thing is summed up by this statement on the cover of the score card:

> When a company hears presentations from as many as 10 dif-
> ferent advertising agencies, it is often helpful to build a profile
> or a checklist of the most important points that should be con-
> sidered. We sincerely hope you agree that the points of strength
> that we have identified in this "Score card" are the principal
> factors to be evaluated as you hear all presentations. (We hope
> you find it useful—and any correlation between these and the
> points that (prospect's name) has used to build its business is
> purely intentional.)

What Do You Leave Behind?

The objective of any presentation is to get the order and the smart agency person will conclude his presentation by boldly asking for the business. You may not get your answer right then and there but it can't hurt to try. If you don't get the business, you'll want to give the prospect some material to keep to remind him or her of you and your presentation while he or she is considering the final choice of agency.

For this purpose many agencies use a written summary of their presen-
tation. It's important that this be a digest of the presentation actually made to the prospect and tailor-made to his or her interests. It should repeat what you've said and not just be a generalized piece about the virtues of your agency. Don't succumb to the temptation to let the prospect see this summary before you've finished your presentation. To do so will just distract him.

Two agencies I know include as the last section of a leave-behind pre-
sentation summary a copy of their standard agency-client agreement which they've already signed. Not only is this a great way to signify your real interest in the prospect's account and ask for the order, but it offers a good handle for the essential follow-up.

Following Up

Each and every contact with a prospect that elicits any degree of interest should be followed up promptly. If your first approach by letter draws a reply, get on the phone right away and press to set up a personal meeting.

When you've been invited to make a formal presentation it's especially important to follow up to see if a decision has been made or if you can supply more information that would be helpful in reaching a decision. One good gambit is to ask if the agreement form you left with the prospect at the end of the presentation has been signed yet or whether it needs some modifications.

If your presentation hasn't brought in the account, it's important to try to find out who did get it and why you didn't. This won't get you the account, but it will help you profit by your mistakes and build a better presentation for the future. Who knows, you may even get a second crack later on at the guy who turned you down.

24

Look Before You Leap

How often have you heard the old cliché, "There's nothing wrong with this agency that a million dollars of billing won't cure"? Sometimes yes, sometimes no.

I think the general principle shoud be that any procedure that brings in profitable and desirable business is good, while activities aimed at increasing billing without these qualifications are likely to be bad. Perhaps you think this is an obvious statement; however, agencies frequently are so desirous of increasing their billing that they wish-think themselves into the conclusion that they make money on practically anything which comes in on top of present billing. This is very far from the truth.

View Some Billing Skeptically

I'm referring to billing from clients who have a legitimate product or service to sell and whose financial responsibility is well established but who, for whatever reason, prefer to operate under unorthodox agency-client relationships. There are two basic types.

Controlled Accounts
Possibly the most common account of this type is business controlled by individuals who peddle it around to agencies placing it with the outfit that offers the best deal, without too much worry about the abilities involved or the appropriateness of the agency for the accounts concerned.

The smart salesperson who peddles this kind of account will tell you the billing is sure to be so many thousands of dollars, and he or she will do all the contact and creative work. All the agency has to do is check the insertions and send out the bills.

Soft pedaled or totally ignored at this time are the facts that the agency is taking a credit risk, that the peddlers will need office space, telephone service, possibly the part-time services of a secretary, and much more time from the other agency executives than is mentioned in the preliminary talks. Nothing is ever said about the real qualifications of the agency to handle the account involved or the possible discontent of the client if the advertising service delivered is not good. And you have no way of judging whether this peddler is a good advertising person or not.

Sometimes this kind of deal works out fine, but in general it is the least desirable new business the agency can get. It rests in one person's pocket; it stays only as long as it is more profitable to its controller than some deal offered by another shop.

Look with suspicion upon any split commission deal. It is generally undesirable from many angles. You have no real hold on any business you do not contact yourself and in which the agency is not functioning creatively.

Cut-Rate Accounts
These are another common cause of agency losses. All sorts of deals are worked out by which, in one way or another, the agency rebates a large portion of the commissions earned. Agency associations endeavored to outlaw the procedure, but were ruled to be in restraint of trade by the federal government.

Agencies, said the ruling, were free to sell their services at any price they considered fair. Consequently, many clients are shopping around and buying their agency services at bargain rates.

You are taking your business life in your hands if you get into any of these cut-rate situations. At cut prices you can't deliver proper services and dissatisfaction is sure to result.

Any deal that departs from the simple bilateral benefit agreement between agency and client should be looked at with suspicion. Basically the client has something to sell and an appropriation for selling it. Some part of this money may well be earned by the agency because of its specialized skills and its facilities for producing the advertising and placing it where it will do the most good.

But any working agreement that cuts down on the service rendered or that reduces the agency's legitimate profit is destined to fail. It is surprising how often this simple fact is ignored and how often arrangements are started that cannot possibly succeed.

When the client buys at cut rates, he never expects the same cut in service. That's invariably what he gets, however. You go all out learning about the client's business, spend far more than you should in time, hoping that it will pay off eventually, but you are so handicapped by too low an income that the client kicks, out goes the account, and the whole operation shows you a serious loss. Far better to insist on remuneration higher than the 15 percent standard, if the account promises to be difficult and requires excessive time to handle properly.

Sad to relate but true, it is almost invariably the agency left holding the bag in these deals and it is the agency that loses the money. Only the agency's capital is used. The client risks nothing financially, although lost sales and reputation may be far more expensive in the long run than has been realized.

Special Projects As a Foot in the Door

In recent years it has become increasingly common for the initial agency-advertiser relationship to be in the form of a special project. Many agencies welcome this technique, which gives them a chance to show what they can do without committing the advertiser to an assignment of his or her whole account.

A good example of how this can benefit an agency was presented by a friend of mine in Texas who took on a special assignment for a local division of a nationwide multi-industry conglomerate. To do the job right he had to visit and work closely with many of the offices of subsidiaries and divisions. What better way to get to know the advertiser's people and gain their confidence? Another agency I know, in Nebraska, told me he got what are now his two largest accounts by handling specialized projects for them and impressing them with what he could do.

Of course, there are dangers in this approach, too. If an agency takes on a succession of special projects for a client, it may acquire the reputation, at least with that advertiser, of being a hotshot bull pen artist who's never given a starting assignment. And it's frustrating to be always putting out fires.

Credit Checks

This may seem redundant in a chapter on looking before leaping, but it's so vital to an agency's very survival that I'm going to say it again. Don't take any business from a client whose credit is doubtful, or, if there is any question about it, get your money before closing dates or other times when your liability begins. Never forget that it's your credit, your capital, and your reputation that are on the line.

The Effect of Client Conflicts

The spate of megamergers in the mid-1980s among both agencies and advertisers has raised a considerable amount of worry in the agency business about client conflicts and the subsequent loss of business. That this is a real cause for concern can be seen from the large-scale client shifts that followed the Saatchi & Saatchi absorption of Ted Bates and the creation of Omnicom by BBDO, Doyle Dayne Bernbach, and Needham, Harper & Steers. According to stories in *Advertising Age*, the volume of billing that changed hands came to more than $372 million.

Some of the details of these account shifts show Saatchi/Bates losing $255 million net and Omnicom losing $117 million net. On the other hand, Young & Rubicam (not merged) gained $254 million net. This frantic activity contrasts sharply with total account shifts of $576.5 million in 1976 and $1.4 billion in 1981.

This kind of account shakeout can redound to your benefit, if you are able to pick up one of the accounts being shed by the mergee. This situation raises two related questions. The first is how to minimize the effect of client conflicts on your agency whether they arise from a merger, from your acquisition of a new account, or from your client's entry into a business competitive with that of one of your other clients. In considering any question of client conflict you must remember that, just as beauty is in the eye of the beholder, a perception of conflict is always in the eye of the client. If he or she thinks it exists, it does whether you think so or not.

If the potential "conflict" results from your taking on a new account, just plain common sense indicates that you should clear with your present client before taking on a new account that might conflict with one of his or her areas of interest to insure, as best you can, that it will not be considered a conflict. It will help him or her make this favorable decision if you have served him or her long and well on your present assignment and he or she is thoroughly convinced of your integrity.

Another positive step you can take to minimize the effects of a possible conflict is to provide that the two potentially conflicting accounts are handled by completely different groups in your office or even in a different office if you have more than one. Some mergers are designed with this possibility in mind.

The second question is whether you should seek out a merger in order to position yourself better to take advantage of this churning of accounts.

Before answering this second question let's first consider the reasons why agencies seek to merge. These, not necessarily in order of importance, are: 1. financial, 2. acquisition of good people, 3. acquisition of new accounts, 4. acquisition of an office in a new territory, and 5. acquisition of a service capability you do not now have, such as direct response or medical advertising.

I would strongly urge you to seek out a merger only if it makes economic sense in view of the above goals. If merging would also help you meet possible conflict situations (for example, by giving you a completely separate office facility), that should be considered a plus value, not a strong reason in itself, for merging.

25

What Do Advertisers Look for in an Agency?

This seems to be a good note on which to conclude this section on new business. Certainly if we know what an advertiser is really looking for, we can prepare and deliver our presentations more intelligently.

Recently I was privileged to sit in on a seminar at which a group of advertising managers told how they had gone about selecting the agencies to which they had recently shifted their accounts.

The first thing each of them did was draw up a list of criteria applicable to his or her particular situation. Three were used by all of them. First, size in relation to his own advertising budget. Each of them was concerned that the agency neither be so large that his or her account would be lost in the shuffle nor so small that his or her account would put a severe strain on the agency's facilities and personnel.

Second, location was a factor in all cases except one which was located in a small city with no agencies of any size. All the ad managers wanted to be sure of getting service when they needed it.

The third common criterion was the experience of the agency. It needn't be in the advertiser's specific industry but should be related. For instance, a manufacturer of snack foods was interested in any kind of package goods background; a bank looked for experience with financial institutions other than banks; a manufacturer of products for the automotive aftermarket wanted experience in marketing brand name merchandise of any sort.

Information of this kind is pretty easy to come by from published sources and was used to narrow down to a manageable number the agencies to be considered.

Some agencies on the final lists may have been known to the advertiser from previous contacts, others by reputation only, but every one of them seemed able to provide what was wanted.

Interesting, isn't it, how these list-building criteria parallel almost exactly the considerations the agency uses in building its own file of likely prospects?

Thus, after narrowing the list of agencies to those he or she believes can do the job, the advertiser sets up a series of more or less formal presentations from each of them. Then he or she makes a choice, which has to be pretty subjective.

Whatever the rationale used by individual advertisers, I think the essential qualities of an agency on which the final selection is based are brain power, good judgment, experience, and intellectual honesty.

What tests can the advertiser apply that will indicate the presence or absence of these essentials in an agency under consideration?

Intelligence

The brain power of an agency, or intelligence, will show up in its type of presentation, its analysis of itself in relation to its future client, and its tact, foreshadowing happy or difficult personal relations to come. One of the participants in the seminar I attended put it this way, "Will this agency-client relationship be a good one four or five years from now?"

The client's response to evident agency intelligence will be, "We like these people. They talk our language. They probably will be able to understand our business. They think about our problems with good common sense. They are not bluffing. We can understand their reasoning."

Intelligence is most frequently tested by the subject's solutions to problems. All those indications listed above, when you think about them, are right or wrong answers to problems.

Intelligence is of surpassing importance as an agency asset. It means much more than cleverness, ingenuity, even more than salesmanship. It is, in an individual, the ability to understand and cope with the difficulties of an environment. Selling is an exercise in understanding and coping with the buying environment. This term means whatever we are surrounded by. In our always expressive slang, whatever we are up against.

Good Judgment

Let's turn now to good judgment. This depends largely on intelligence, but it goes further by also involving the understanding of people and the ability to interpret events. Essentially, in the agency-client relationship, good judgment will show up in recommendations regarding business policy. Here the advertiser must beware of the human weakness of considering as correct the judgment with which he or she agrees. The advertiser must be very open-minded in recognizing and giving proper consideration to judgment that differs from his or her own.

One of the seminar panelists selected his new agency when he felt he could answer yes to the question, "Would we have the guts to follow really significant, substantial, meaty recommendations from this person?" That the advertiser could even formulate this question to himself demonstrates clearly his conviction that the agency possessed good judgment.

Experience

The next basic quality to look for is experience. By this I mean general business experience, not necessarily experience in the prospect's own business. Much might be said for the uncluttered mind that comes fresh to a business problem, without preconceived ideas based on "this is the way we have always done it."

Experience in advertising usually is demonstrated by materials illustrating what the agency has done for others. Here it is difficult to segregate the agency's contribution from that which may have come from the client. A series of case histories of accounts that have shown increased sales and bigger profits during the agency's tenure is as good an indication of agency experience as any. Mistrust any case histories of failures. They may or may not have been the agency's fault. Also mistrust the agency that, in its case histories, claims credit for every success the client ever had. Nobody is that good.

Intellectual Honesty

And finally we come to intellectual honesty. Of all the forms of honesty, this is the rarest and most to be desired when one is considering an adviser. Monetary honesty we expect; individuals and corporations have learned it is dangerous not to practice it. Intellectual honesty is the ability to think straight and the courage to say what you think. It's the integrity to admit, for example, that extra media spending is not the answer to every problem.

When an agency demonstrates this kind of honesty a whole batch of possible minor faults can be discounted, for this is the most desirable and rarest trait in an adviser. When combined with intelligence and experience it's the answer to an advertiser's prayer.

Many readers may accuse me of leaving out the desirable feature of compatibility. Well, it's nice to be married to a concern you like, with which you get along, and whose background and experience in life are akin to yours. It's much more important, however, for the agency to have the client's respect and to be able to give him or her real help.

What about creativity? Don't prospects look for evidence of that in an agency? I left it out deliberately because I don't think you can define creativity in terms that make sense at the time of a presentation. Just as the proof of the pudding is in the eating, the proof of creativity is in the results accomplished. And that's mighty hard to demonstrate in a presentation.

I don't think it's as important for the prospect to look for the ability to produce good advertising as it is to find the personal characteristics without which good advertising cannot be created. You do not, says the old English proverb, make silk purses out of sows' ears. It's quite possible that the client doesn't possess the ability to spot and appreciate good advertising. As a good businessperson, however, he or she should possess the ability to evaluate the human powers behind good advertising. He or she should pick an agency that evidently has brain power, judgment, experience, and intellectual honesty; he or she shouldn't try to think for it but leave it alone to give the best it can. The results of this philosophy should be a satisfying and rewarding relationship for both parties.

VI Some General Observations

26

What It Takes to Succeed

All through this book there have been suggestions on how to run an agency successfully. They cover a lot of different details, so it may be well to summarize here what I call the *10 Point Formula for Agency Success*.

Here, based on a great many years of running and advising agencies, are the components that, if strictly complied with by people whose characteristics and talents are as described, will be found to work.

Honesty

Are you surprised to find this at the head of the list? Fact is, it is the single most important·ingredient in the mix. This is because advertising agencies are trusted advisors to advertisers, who put large sums of money in the agencies' hands and have every right to expect that it will be expended properly. These advertisers ask for guidance in a difficult field, where many things are matters of conjecture, where results are far off in time and locale.

I'm not speaking of the alliances that last only a short time, but of those agency-client relationships which may last many years. (The short-term ones soon correct themselves.) Here, in these frequent and richly productive partnerships between the advertiser and the agency, honesty on both sides is a must. Without it, the deal is doomed almost before it starts.

Ability

No agency lasts long or has a chance for real success unless it knows its business. An agency must be rich in creative ability, in marketing savvy, in knowledge of people, in economics, and in a dozen or so other things you can list as well as I.

Fundamentally an agency is hired and earns its gross income because it knows more about these things than the client does, who presumably has plenty on his mind understanding and mastering his own business.

Salesmanship

That means for the agency itself, and for the clients. This is a peculiar and extrovert ability not all people or companies possess. You have to understand folks and like them. You have to be able to put yourself in their shoes. You have to have the arguments and the personality to make someone else believe what you say and do what you recommend.

Attitude

This means clients first, their interests before those of the agency. Of course, any agency which possesses this proper feeling toward the companies which trust it with cash money will do credit to themselves without any further effort. But this attitude is rarer than you might think.

Management

This, in the agency, means many things. It is concerned with the personnel of the agency, with financial matters, and with proper work distribution and allocation.

Management manages both money and people. It has to have horse sense. It has to look far ahead. It needs many attitudes quite foreign to, and usually beyond, the abilities of creative and imaginative advertising brains. It insists on knowing where it is going and how and when and often *why*.

It's easy to see why it is difficult for agency people to be good business managers. Fundamentally we are creative critters. We are salespeople. We are communicators of mercantile information. To do these jobs well we must be enthusiastic, able to put ourselves into the other fellow's shoes, sympathetic and understanding of the reactions and attitudes of other people. These characteristics would seem to be almost diametrically opposed to those required of a typical, efficient business manager. So the functions of creation and those of management must always be performed by two separate people.

Because we're a people business, management of an advertising agency requires, either in the principals or in some associated individual, personnel handling as well as financial abilities. The person called on to function in these hard-boiled realities of figures and human reactions must possess good business judgment, extending to both events and personalities. He or she must be a good and accurate judge of facts and people. This individual must possess, most of all, good horse sense. He or she must be a realist par excellence. Lack of realism and common sense is one of the most frequent causes of agency failure.

Money

An agency needs enough to start with, including a generous margin of safety to provide for delays in payment and unexpected early setbacks (before it is familiar with these regular phenomena), enough to establish credit, take cash discounts, and most of all, avoid lying awake nights worrying where the payroll is coming from.

It needs to build this working capital out of profits and increase it steadily as the years go on and the financial jobs get bigger. It needs to invest surpluses wisely, so they earn their part in the gross income. It needs to pay its people well, not only today, but in the future also, when they will need more income.

Escape Hatches

Escape hatches are provisions against the unexpected. Agencies must set up ways to survive adversity. They must build their storm cellars in the sure realization that fair weather never lasts forever and that the country in which we are living and working is particularly prone to extreme atmospheric disturbances. These safety provisions may be in the form of insurance. One need not detail them. Sufficient to say, we must have them storing up the corn of the fat years to provide against the lean years so lamentably sure to come.

One of the most important reverses against which protection is needed is the all-too-frequent case in which the client cuts his budget, but doesn't reduce proportionately his needs for service. Agencies can adjust to this situation if given some time in which to turn around.

Two agencies I know have bought this time by including what they call "disaster clauses" in their client contracts. Here they are.

The first one (in a fee contract) reads:

> In the event the budget is reduced 10% or more, the Company agrees to continue, for a three-month period, the monthly fee which was in effect when the reduction was made. During this three-month period the Agency will adjust manpower requirements as necessary to provide the required service.

The second one (in all contracts) reads:

> Should the Client drastically reduce or cancel space contracts after approving the advertising schedules and after the Agency has done much of its work, the Client agrees to accept Agency billings in the amount of the commissions the Agency would have received for the schedules originally approved.

Adjustable Executive Capacity

This category really falls under management, but it is so seldom provided for that it rates a separate heading. What is meant is planning for and coping with the time, which always comes as the small agency grows, when one man's time and effort are inadequate to handle the growing responsibilities of more and bigger business.

Most agency heads are so busy working at their jobs that this contingency hits them unexpectedly, and they begin to run around wondering whether they should hire more people, merge with another agency, or provide on the shortest notice the most difficult of all commodities to find—able and experienced people.

These most important needs must be anticipated and provided for in advance. Second- and indeed third-string understudies should be in training continually. The wise manager always has a relief pitcher warming up in the bull pen.

Constant New Business Activity

Most agencies begin to scurry around for business only when their billings drop or some account needs to be replaced. Part of the formula of every successful agency is constant selling of the agency itself, by mail, by telephone, and in person.

Unless you figure that account mortality is inevitable you are in danger. Insist on agency growth, every year if possible, or know why not.

Happiness

Run a happy shop that no one wants to leave, or your shop will leave you. Beat your people to the punch on all matters affecting their own welfare, particularly monetary. Especially in our sensitive, temperamental business this is of vital importance. Injustice, exploitation, too big a break for the boss, unkept promises, actual or implied—these are the cancers that spell death to any agency.

So, success (in the true sense of the word) boils down to ability, experience, and character.

27

The Place of Psychology in Advertising

[Reprinted, with permission of Harper & Row, Publishers, from *Advertising Agency Success* by Kenneth Groesbeck]

Every good advertising man or woman is instinctively a sound psychologist. The creator of advertising may know nothing of psychological terms, may be completely unaware of the processes of his or her own mind, but when the successful advertisement or campaign is examined by a qualified psychologist and all its characteristics are set down and given their correct and technical names, the thinking behind the campaign will turn out to be in accordance with correct psychological principles.

What use is it, then, for the advertising agency person to know something about psychology in advance? Such a knowledge may help toward sound thinking and logical reasoning. It may cause him or her to discard appeals that may have seemed attractive and direct him toward appeals that formal psychology knows to be correct.

If knowledge of psychology causes an advertising person to produce better advertising, then such knowledge is a valuable asset. If it is going to confuse him, however—cause him to substitute rules and regulations for true creation—quite possibly the less he knows about it the better.

Perhaps psychology should be seen and not heard. Seen by the agency, but not too obtrusively thrust upon the client unless he or she asks for it. Seen to the extent that some knowledge of the subject on the agency's part may serve to back up and confirm its sound selling instincts and experience. One doubts that the old masters of advertising could cite you paragraph or verse of psychological doctrine, but they were sound psychologists at that.

The Problem of Communication

We may safely start with the assumption that any effective communication—and that is the soul of all creative effort in every field—is based on a correct approach to the human mind.

Psychology recognizes that communication travels from the originator through his or her medium (art, music, teaching, public speaking, the written word, pictures, advertising, for example) to the recipient. Once that is stated, your reaction is, "Well, of course I knew that."

Perhaps you knew it, but to what degree have you acted upon it? How much have you been aware that a successful communication must travel? How much have you thought about the means that will speed it on its way?

Do we not too often produce an advertisement that is pleasing to ourselves, is unusual, striking, or beautiful without asking ourselves, "How fast will this message travel, how easily will it be transmitted, how surely will it reach its destination?" All those thoughts should occur to us as we begin to study psychology, and note the travel element involved in communication.

The Receiving Mind

The next thing that psychology tells us is that reception may be blocked by a mind that is opposed, uninterested, lazy, or tired. It finds these unfavorable attitudes, and the favorable ones as well, in what is technically called the *apperceptive mass*. This consists of our memories and our experiences as they have been digested by our minds.

Psychology points out the need for creating attention before the message has any chance to get across. This result, when it happens, is called perception.

The science now notes that it is not enough to obtain perception. It finds that once the impression has been received, it may be unfavorably regarded and immediately thrown out by the mind. So it asks us to make sure that what is perceived shall be agreeable to the recipient.

That it may be so, psychology warns us to be aware of habit, preconceptions, and prejudices. Perceptions are more readily welcomed when they coincide with human impressions already received that are of an agreeable nature.

Next, psychology dwells on what is called comprehension and remarks that it is no use getting an impression through if the mind cannot understand it after it has been received. Even if the message is understood—and this is of special interest to advertising people—there is an additional wide step remaining between conviction and action.

Psychology helps us to understand how the mind receives impressions through the senses, how it interprets these impressions, how it utilizes them in the formation of opinions and in the regulation of actions.

Our Mental Bombardment

The mind is constantly receiving messages of all sorts and from hundreds of sources. We see, hear, smell, feel, and are otherwise aware of all sorts of external conditions. To most of these stimuli we are impervious. Only the strongest have a chance to make any impression upon us.

We receive and take note of any messages that concern our personal safety and welfare. This is instinctive and helps toward self-preservation. We are aware when it is hot or when it is cold; when the sun is shining and when it is raining; whether or not the pavement is slippery; where and how fast automobiles are moving, and other people as well; and we hear sounds designed to warn us in advance of any danger.

The mind does not reason about these things; it maintains an awareness of them and automatically acts in response to them in a way calculated to keep us comfortable and safe. Such stimuli are subconsciously marked, as it were, as of primary importance.

Second to them come stimuli such as those that surround us in the safety of our homes or those that impinge upon us when someone speaks to us. Such stimuli receive more or less attention depending upon the character of the individual and the importance of the message conveyed. Still another classification of outside impulses that our minds allow to enter are those that come from our amusements, our reading, our radio and television hearing and watching, and the like. Such stimuli are voluntarily sought and should be correspondingly welcome.

This must make us realize how busy the human mind is receiving and assimilating; first, the stimuli necessary for existence; second, those external impressions that are thrust upon us by our environment; and third, those which are voluntarily accepted by us for amusement, entertainment, or education.

Raising the Stature of Advertising

One may well wonder, when one realizes how busy the human mind is taking care of these external impressions, what chance advertising has to make an impression. Here a knowledge of psychology can be a help to us. It may teach us how to shape our advertising impressions so that they partake of the sharpness and importunity of self-preservation impulses.

At first thought you may doubt that advertising impressions can be raised to the stature of self-preservation stimuli. However, if you will remember that we have other things to preserve as well as our lives, you may become aware that we also need to preserve our self-respect, our social standing, our pride, and our happiness. These things may not be as important as our lives, but they are important enough to us to justify basing advertising appeals on them.

What is a good advertising man or woman doing when basing his or her appeal upon some well-known, so-called line of least resistance to the human mind? He or she is raising an otherwise commonplace appeal to the height of those that demand attention because of their bearing upon survival. Remember that by this we mean not only life; we mean also the other things that make life worth living.

Conscious and Subconscious

Psychology notes that the mind seems to be a double-barrelled affair consisting of the conscious and the subconscious mind. This last is something of a mystery. We know it is there because we see it in action — particularly when we let a problem simmer in our heads for days or even weeks, and suddenly, from somewhere, up pops the solution.

Most of us, tackling a creative problem, work hard and continuously at it and frequently end up against a sort of barrier. The thing just won't jell. In desperation, often against a deadline, we push harder and harder, and still we seem to be stumped.

So we do the best we can and the job goes through, often fairly well-done. But inevitably we say to ourselves, "Somehow that thing could have been done better." There is something beyond what has been accomplished. Why couldn't we get through to that perfect performance which, theoretically, we know to be possible?

When this happens to us we have been shooting with only one barrel of our minds. The second barrel is, of course, the subconscious. It is nothing new to say that it is there and that it is more efficient than our conscious mind. The trouble is we are seldom told how we can make it work.

Putting the Subconscious to Work

There is a definite technique for using the subconscious. Step one is to saturate ourselves thoroughly with a problem and solve it in as many ways as possible. From an advertising standpoint this, of course, means finding out all about the background of the product or service, examining its past advertising, competitive advertising, and its marketing procedure. Every advertising man or woman is thoroughly familiar with these preliminaries. None of us would be so foolish as to begin to think about advertising slants and copy until we have given ourselves this thorough indoctrination.

As we do this sort of digging, jotting down ideas as we go, we may come upon the approach we want, which will be new, probably different, sound, adapted to the reader or hearer, simple and convincing. If so, fine!

On the other hand the abler we are, the more critical we are of what we have produced. Here is the crucial point in the process. Right here we do one of two things. Either we let it go or we push harder than ever. The better we are, the more apt we are to do the latter. That is where we make our mistake.

Arrived at this mental sound barrier, having pushed our conscious minds to the limit, we should now change our tactics.

We should deliberately say to our subconscious minds, "Take it from here." From this point on for several days—or even weeks—we stop pressing. All we do is occasionally think consciously of the problem.

This seems to give the subconscious a prod, somehow. Above all, we must not push the process. It's a sort of incubation period. It takes time, and it takes a degree of repose, so far as the conscious is concerned. If we keep on worrying about the job, which is a conscious mind activity, we are spurring the wrong horse. We have already tried this to the limit and it doesn't work. If we fret and stew about the thing, we will not only get nowhere with our conscious minds, we will definitely handicap the subconscious activity.

There is no objection if we occasionally ask the subconscious, "How are you doing?" But beyond this, we must mentally do nothing.

The next thing to be sure of is that we always have by us a little notebook and a pencil. This should be with us by day, and beside our beds at night because there is no telling when the marvel-working subconscious will blandly come up with the solution, and sit back grinning at us because we didn't think of that one.

Our subconscious minds seem to enjoy solving problems at inconvenient times. These may be when we are trying to sleep, when we are in the shower, or when we are walking along the street. This is not too difficult to understand.

It is because at these times our minds are relaxed, thinking of nothing in particular. Nothing is blocking the subconscious process. So frequently we outline an entire advertising campaign with one side of our face shaved. We know from sad experience that if we wait to shave the other half, the idea may be lost.

There are three things to remember. First, saturate yourself with the problem. Second, don't press, for the subconscious has taken over the job. Third, give it time.

Perhaps that sounds unbelievably simple. Nevertheless, psychologically it is sound, and it works.

Motivation Research

One of the newly developed psychological methods concerns itself with human motivations. It asks not what people do, but why they think and act as they do.

One of the most significant findings that has come out of motivation research is that people cannot tell you accurately why they act. They have been motivated by their emotions or unconsciously by some of the output of the apperceptive mass which we have mentioned.

One may get into a considerable tangle, trying to dissociate the accredited reasons from the real ones. These actual motivations, however, are extremely important and it is necessary to uncover them for they indicate the only lines along which a promotion can succeed.

When we study the procedure involved in any motivational research, we see how the trained researcher gets at these real reasons for conviction and action. And it is always astonishing to discover how far apart the real reasons are from those stated by the person being interviewed.

Watch a shopper in a supermarket going down the aisle with a cart and quickly picking certain products. There is no apparent investigation, no evident doubt. These selections are the result of habit and preconceptions built out of experience.

Why does he or she occasionally stop and examine a new product, read its package message carefully, turn it over and over, and note if the contents show through? This product belongs to a class which the person needs, and the individual product concerned is either new or in mental competition with similar products with which perhaps he or she has not been entirely satisfied. Possibly the competing product has been difficult to get out of the package or difficult to use. Perhaps it has failed in the flavor or behavior he or she would consider desirable.

Desirable Product Image

These deeply buried impressions are what motivation research tries to locate and understand. Ask a woman why she picked a certain new product, and she cannot tell you. "I thought I would like it," she answers. Then the researcher begins to probe into her previous experiences with similar products, and in time, out come the real reasons for the switch.

All this is psychology in action. Such a specialized procedure as that of motivational research may have been instinctively practiced by the skilled producer of advertising. Even such an individual, however, is more likely to think correctly if he or she has some knowledge of these mental processes.

Creative people frequently complain that too much research, psychological or otherwise, hampers promotional thinking. It should not. It should clarify it, inspire it, and assure its correctness. One suspects that many such objections come from sheer laziness and the reluctance to become involved in what is conceivably a difficult field.

There is a definite mechanism behind all art, including that of communication. But the highest art conceals itself, leaving only the impression it seeks to create. We know how disappointed we are when an advertisement is admired for itself, rather than approved by the impression it creates and the action it causes.

Psychology discovers and lays down the rules and regulations by which the human mind works. With such knowledge we are more likely to succeed in penetrating the minds we seek to influence than if we proceed entirely by trial and error, or even with the aid of skill and experience.

Put Yourself in His Place

This title of Charles Reade's famous old novel is a psychological fundamental of good advertising, and indeed of all effective communication.

The ability to project ourselves into the minds of our listeners may be instinctive in some people. These, one supposes, are what are called good mixers. With most of us the ability is an acquired one because it requires a subordination of our own personality, which is contrary to what we instinctively wish to do.

Fundamentally we like to think about ourselves and in terms of ourselves. A good advertising person, however, thinks in terms of others. When writing he or she thinks not of the content per se, but of the impression the writing will make upon the mind of the person receiving the message.

Great artists and great actors possess this ability instinctively. They transfer themselves wholly into the minds of their audience. They are concerned not with what they are, but with what their hearers are thinking them to be.

To make this transfer effectively, we must possess a high degree of imagination. We must see the product not as it stands upon the shelves of the retail store, but as it is behaving in the hands of its users.

It is difficult for an individual to effect this transference of himself into the minds of others unless he has a thorough understanding of the thoughts and emotions of other people and is completely in sympathy with them.

Any attempt to assume this sympathy and understanding will fail. If you do not sincerely believe in a product or a service yourself, you are unlikely to be able to write about it or talk about it convincingly. If you are not willing to realize how much more important the product is in the mind of the user than it is in your own mind, you are struggling against a well-nigh insuperable obstacle.

A knowledge of psychology can help us to this sympathy and understanding. It will not secure it for us however, until we are willing to abandon our interest in ourselves and substitute an overriding interest in the mental reactions of others.

28
Advertising Agencies in a Recession

At various places in this book, and particularly in the first section, I've discussed at length some of the characteristics of the advertising agency business that tend to make it a risky and unpredictable one—low profit margins, temperamental personnel, fickle clients, and so forth. At first glance, this might make it seem that advertising agencies would be particularly vulnerable in times of a decline in general business activity.

There are, however, a lot of characteristics of the agency business that tend to temper the effects of a recession on a well-managed, hard-working agency. Since I am a firm believer in advertising and agencies, after devoting a lifetime to the business, I think it highly appropriate to conclude this book on a positive note by pointing out some of these plus values.

Advertising Is Increasing

Back in 1962 *Printer's Ink* carried a feature article, provocatively entitled "How to Advertise out of a Recession," in its November 2 issue. I obtained a copy and found several interesting charts that showed that advertising volume hit a low during the depression year 1933 and then increased almost without interruption every year thereafter.

This started me on a search for more data that culminated in the August 27, 1973 issue of *Advertising Age* where estimated advertising expenditures were listed for every year from 1935 to 1972. Other articles have made it possible to extend the data as far as 1986.

For the entire 51-year period, total advertising expenditures have increased on an average of 8.53 percent each year. What's more, the year-to-year spending has increased 48 times and decreased only three — in 1938, 1942, and 1961. It seems that advertising tends to keep on increasing in dollar volume almost regardless of the general state of the economy. There are many reasons for this but one of the main ones is undoubtedly that expressed in an *Advertising Age* story about Warner-Lambert (March 3, 1975, p. 2) which says "Today's economy provides a golden opportunity for a company to protect its franchises . . . . While companies that can't afford to support their products retrench, financially sound companies can strengthen their holds on the market. This is exactly what Warner-Lambert plans to do . . . . W-L will increase advertising expenditures in 1975."

Agencies Are Growing

Fine, you say, total advertising is increasing but how do individual agencies come out? To find an answer to this question I studied the comparative billing figures that *Advertising Age* publishes each year for many hundreds of agencies. I looked at the reports published for every year since 1972, a period that experienced both ups and downs in general business, and this is what I found:

	Changes in Individual Agency Billing (1972–1975) Or Gross Income (1976 et seq.)		
Year	Agencies Included	Percent Growing	Average Increase
1972	583	84.56%	15.70%
1973	634	83.60	15.10
1974	576	88.02	8.79
1975	648	75.46	10.40
1976	587	86.20	18.38
1977	520	89.42	18.26
1978	597	91.12	18.87
1979	634	89.43	18.62
1980	707	85.29	18.20
1981	776	87.76	18.93
1982	772	81.09	24.40
1983	784	83.80	14.50
1984	589	92.24	18.73
1985	660	85.76	15.25
1986	526	80.61	11.80

In each of these years an overwhelming percentage of individual agencies increased their billing (or gross income) as compared to the year before. What's more, the results were almost the same for agencies in all size groups.

The average size of the increase in billing (or gross income) is a very respectable 16.72 percent over the entire period, determined after eliminating the highest tenth and the lowest tenth. The resulting average, which our statistical friends would call an inter-decile average, thus represents a reliable indicator as to what a typical agency actually did.

Agencies Serve a Diversified Clientele

It's extremely unlikely that all parts of the nation's economy will be affected the same way or to the same degree in what's commonly called a recession. Recently, for example, fuel oil is down but coal is up; industrial trucks are up but materials handling equipment is down; refrigerators are down but freezers are up; beer is up and whiskey is down.

Most agencies have pretty widely diversified client lists and this gives them some degree of protection against disastrous declines in income. The members of First Advertising Agency Network, who typically represent small- to medium-sized agencies, have between them clients in 379 of the 958 industries listed in the Standard Industrial Classification Manual. That's just under 40 percent of the total. What's more, the individual members served clients in an average of 25 different industries. The chances of all, or even most, of these going sour at the same time are pretty remote.

New Products Are Continually Introduced

In times of recession as well as in boom times American advertisers are forever adding new products to their lines. To realize the extent of this activity all you have to do is read the newspapers and magazines and note all the new improved widgets or the revolutionary advances in detergents advertised there. It is an exercise in futility even to try to compile a list that would be anywhere near complete.

Each of these introductions involves substantial amounts of advertising. The stories in *Advertising Age* carry such headlines as "hefty ad backing," "big budget set," "heavy push," "hefty tv, radio effort."

New Accounts Are Available

One of the hazards of the agency business that I pointed out in an earlier section is the frequent turnover in accounts. This is still a fact of life for agencies but it can be a source of hope as well as despair. Don't forget that every time an agency loses an account another agency gains one.

This switching of accounts goes on all the time—in good times as well as bad—maybe even more in hard times because some advertisers have an unfortunate tendency to fire an agency when sales fall off.

A smart, capable agency principal who runs a sound new business operation on a regular basis will undoubtedly gain more than he or she will lose in this kind of situation. The new clients are out there if you just keep beating the bushes.

Expenses Are Controllable

By its very nature most of the expenses an advertising agency incurs are variable and generally it has very little capital tied up in fixed assets.

If you refer back to chapter 5, you'll see that payroll accounts for 71.29 percent of our agency's expenses and other expenses account for 28.71 percent. Within reasonably broad limits payroll can be adjusted, particularly when you remember that for agencies with gross income up to about $1.5 million the portion of total payroll that goes to the bosses or principal owners normally runs between 20 percent and 40 percent.

Of the 28.71 percent of nonpayroll expense the largest single item is normally rent (or the operating expenses of a building, if the agency owns its own) which runs about 7 percent to 9 percent of gross income. This is about the only item of nonpayroll expense that is fixed in amount.

All in all, the operating expenses of an advertising agency are highly controllable and can be reduced drastically if necessary to combat bad times. It may not be pleasant to scrimp and save and to work a lot harder than normal but it is possible, and most agency people would be glad to do it for the sake of survival.

Conclusion

While the advertising agency business is not recession-proof, its basic nature is such that it can react to adversity much more rapidly and positively than can most businesses.

The total volume of advertising keeps on increasing steadily in good years and bad — in 48 out of the last 51 years to be exact — and in this atmosphere there's business to be had by the smart, aggressive, well-managed agency even if it has to take some away from a competitor. Advertising is an intangible but vital factor in the business world; it is continually changing to meet new conditions, but, as an industry, it's in no danger of becoming obsolete and disappearing like the manufacture of buggy whips. All in all, it's a business with great potential for the smart, sound agency professional.

Index